PAUL McKENDRICK

THE BUSHMAN'S LAIR

On the Trail of the
Fugitive of the Shuswap

Harbour Publishing Co. Ltd.
P.O. Box 219, Madeira Park, BC, VON 2H0
www.harbourpublishing.com

Edited by Peter Norman
Cover design by Anna Comfort O'Keeffe
Text design by Onça Publishing
Maps by Roger Handling, Terra Firma Design
Printed and bound in Canada
Printed on paper certified by the Forest Stewardship Council

Harbour Publishing acknowledges the support of the Canada Council for the Arts, the Government of Canada, and the Province of British Columbia through the BC Arts Council.

Library and Archives Canada Cataloguing in Publication

Title: The Bushman's lair : on the trail of the fugitive of the Shuswap / Paul McKendrick.
Names: McKendrick, Paul, 1976- author.
Identifiers: Canadiana (print) 20210100753 | Canadiana (ebook) 20210101067 | ISBN 9781550179224 (softcover) | ISBN 9781550179231 (EPUB)
Subjects: LCSH: Bjornstrom, John. | LCSH: Fugitives from justice—British Columbia—Shuswap Lake Region. | LCSH: Thieves—British Columbia—Biography. | LCSH: Escaped prisoners—British Columbia. | LCGFT: Biographies. | LCGFT: True crime stories.
Classification: LCC HV6653.B56 M35 2021 | DDC 364.16/22092—dc23

The Bushman of the Shuswap had a scruffy, bushy beard
He'd haunt the shores of the great lake, he'd steal your fishing gear
Might take your wooden paddles and launch your red canoe
Might wear your hippie sandals and take your gumboots too

The man they called the Bushman would take your summer clothes
Put on your cottage underwear and might borrow your favourite robe
The legend of the Bushman will be told for years to come
And when he's finished doin' his time, he'll be back to roam his kingdom

If your bathing suit's gone missing, if your marshmallows are gone
If your motorboat's gone fishin', then the Bushman's been around
If your neighbor's axe has disappeared, if someone broke the gate
Then you better accept this simple fact, it's the Bushman from the lake

Now he had the cops a hoppin', he was the invisible man
Every time they thought they had him, he'd vanish in the quicksand
He'd taunt those doughnut dunkers by showing up on TV
He would show the young reporter where he slept up in a tree

Yeah, the Bushman wanted to live in Hollywood it seems
And in the end it was the bright lights that brought him down from
    the trees
He spoke about conspiracies, some gold mine called Bre-X
But that's another story, that story cost me ten grand

And if one day when you're down at your cottage by the lake
If you find your bed's been slept in, if there's food left on a plate
If your waffle iron's hissing, can't find your favourite rake
Then you better accept this simple fact, it's the Bushman from the lake

"Bushman of the Shuswap," written and performed by
Charlie Mackenzie

CONTENTS

MAPS

SOUTHERN BRITISH COLUMBIA

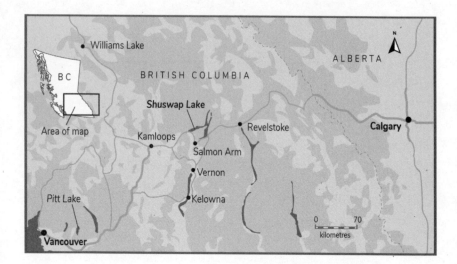

CHAPTER 1

BENEATH THE SURFACE

Submerging a canoe is not very difficult: it can be tilted to one side to let the water pour in. That leaves it floating barely below the surface, assuming it's been constructed from materials that are sufficiently buoyant. If one desires to go further and actually sink the canoe, a dozen or so grapefruit-sized rocks should do the trick. The boat will gradually settle to the bottom. It may still be visible, however, so if the ultimate objective is to conceal its presence, it helps to paint it so that it's indistinguishable from whatever else rests below.

Retrieving a sunken canoe is more burdensome. First, it must be located, which can be hindered by a steep drop-off below the surface or a camouflaging coat of paint. Then it can be fished out with something like a long pole with a hook at one end or, if a suitable jig is unavailable, dragged to the surface by hand. Once the rocks are removed, there's the awkward process of hauling it ashore or finding a sturdy platform to rest one end on, then raising the other end above the water and corkscrewing the boat in midair gracefully enough that no water re-enters before it's returned to an upright and ready position.

The Bushman had carried out the process many times. Although his five-foot-four, two-hundred-pound frame didn't grant him a long reach, his stoutness did facilitate heavy lifting. He hadn't found a way to do the job without getting wet, but the process had become as mindless as driving one's car out of the garage. So inconvenience was not top of mind as he retrieved his canoe from the lake bottom one frigid day in November 2001. It helped that it was daytime—usually he operated under the cover of darkness. But what really kept him from dwelling upon the task was concern that he might be about to walk—or more precisely, canoe—into a trap.

The following summer, near that same spot, a group of house-boaters pulled their rented floating homes, *Yachts of Fun* and *Peat's Pride*, up to a remote beach on British Columbia's Shuswap Lake. The boats were staked to the ground to make sure they stayed put for the night. The beach was equipped with fire pits, but the houseboaters hadn't brought firewood. Collecting dead-wood was prohibited—this beach was within a newly formed provincial park—and a sign on the beach indicated the fine was somewhere in the vast range of $86 to $1,000,000 (the upper end presumably reserved for those pillaging more than a few sticks for a fire).

The law-abiding boaters appointed a three-man crew to harvest fuel farther south down the lake, past the protected area, and they set out in a smaller boat that had been towed behind one of the motherships. They hoped to find large pieces of deadwood floating in the water; this would serve the dual benefits of burning longer into the night and removing the boating hazard. But the lake's waterline had receded in the summer heat, exposing more of the craggy shoreline and leaving less deadwood in the water, so they had to go ashore instead.

Above them rose steep and seemingly impenetrable slopes clad in spruce, fir, cedar and hemlock—an unlikely location for signs of human activity. So they were surprised to see that the receding water had exposed a black hose that snaked under rocks and led up into the bush. They decided to follow it and discovered a faint trail that meandered from above the rocky shoreline and up a couple of switchbacks. They came to what looked like a small wooden shed built into the steep, mossy hillside. It was framed with two-by-eights that didn't yet display the silvery patina of years of oxidation and sun exposure. Fringes of vapor barrier could be seen at junctures in the framing. When the foragers opened the door and poked their heads inside, they were greeted by the beginning of a passageway that disappeared into darkness.

Conveniently there was a light switch just beyond the entranceway, and it illuminated more of the dank corridor. The walls, which looked hastily assembled and suspect in their ability to resist a cave-in, were lined with wood framing intermeshed with wiring and cords. The floor was mostly bare earth, strewn with buckets, pipes and boards. Near the entrance was a smaller portal with a door open just enough to admit the black hose from the lake. The outside of the door was camouflaged with branches held in place by spray insulation. Binoculars hung nearby, presumably used to scan activity on the water.

Farther along, the walls were adorned with snowshoes, fishing nets and other paraphernalia hanging from hooks, and beyond that the passageway broadened to about fifteen feet wide to accommodate a kitchen. Plywood shelves were lined with jars of ground coffee, vegetable oil, sugar, salt and popcorn seeds. There were pots and pans and cleaning supplies, including a fresh box of sos pads. An empty Kraft Dinner box lay beside a well-used two-burner camp stove. Shelves adjacent to the kitchen held a bank of at least ten car batteries interconnected by rusty cables and grounded to a post. A small clothes washer was plugged into the battery bank. Farther along, the passageway was partly obstructed by hundred-pound propane tanks that would weigh about 170 pounds when full.

At the end of the passageway, about thirty feet into the rock, the cave pivoted to the right and expanded into a roughly thirteen-by-thirteen-foot chamber. The space was framed in and protected from moisture by layers of vapour barrier with insulation sandwiched between. An elevated plywood frame supported a regular bed mattress upon which lay an assortment of blankets and clothing. Storage units fashioned from plywood surrounded the bed. Wiring that fed into the bedroom was connected to various lights, a computer and a radio. Reading material was scattered about, including a newspaper opened to an article on Osama bin Laden. In the corner stood a small bird cage, though nothing stared back at them from it.

The boaters asked themselves whose abode it could be. An especially private hermit? Someone with an unorthodox idea of a fishing lodge? Or perhaps someone more menacing who could return at any moment? They didn't linger to find out. They returned to their group to tell them of their discovery and informed the manager of the houseboat rental company, who had shown up to fix a faulty battery in one of the boats.

The manager needed few details to identify the occupant: "It's the home of the Shuswap Bushman!"

While travelling the large body of water nocturnally by canoe and helping himself to provisions from cabins in the area, the Bushman had built the nine-hundred-square-foot cave and furnished it with supplies from those same cabins. After the houseboat manager was shown the cave, he radioed the police. They appeared shortly thereafter, questioned the houseboaters, appropriated film from their cameras and began removing the stolen possessions from the cave to be floated down the lake on a barge. The houseboaters, meanwhile, finished their holiday and set off on the five-hour journey to return their floating homes to their moorage. Along the way they were intercepted and boarded by a TV news reporter and cameraman eager to learn more about the Bushman's hideout.

The Bushman had already garnered a following as the result of earlier media coverage of his escapades. But many viewed the coverage as glamourizing. "I hate it when people call him the Bushman," said one police staffer. "He's just a two-bit crook." The police sergeant tasked with bringing him in echoed that comment: "Let's not romanticize this guy. He's a thief. Sure, he's a bizarre thief. But he's a thief." Some cabin owners recoiled at any suggestion that he was anything more than a "bush rat" or "garbage bear." And a local newspaper questioned the idea that he was some kind of Robin Hood and instead referred to him as "just a loser who's lost in the woods."

CHAPTER 2

INTO THE DARK

> ◀◀ Possibly, then, writing has to do with darkness, and a desire or perhaps a compulsion to enter it, and, with luck, to illuminate it, and to bring something back out to the light."
>
> **Margaret Atwood**, *Negotiating with the Dead: A Writer on Writing*

Shuswap Lake has four arms of unequal length that give it the shape of a lopsided H. The southwestern arms that form the bottom half of the H are home to towns, farms and industry amid a landscape ranging from rolling grasslands sprinkled with ponderosa pine to fertile farmland incised by meandering waterways and flanked by evergreen hills. In contrast, the top half of the H is more inaccessible and untamed. Towering alpine peaks capture moisture from the Pacific, sustaining the unique inland rainforest ecosystem below and building up large snowpacks in the winter that replenish the lake, which in some parts is over five hundred feet deep.

Having four arms makes the lake attractive for tourism. Not only does the elongated shape provide more explorable shoreline—the reported length of which ranges from over 1,400 kilometres to a more credible 405 kilometres, depending on the source—but it also provides four different destinations. This is particularly attractive to houseboaters who want to feel they are captains of their own ships and not just on the same journey as the other roughly two hundred houseboats that could be plying the waters at the same time. Of course, they need not leave the comforts of their lavish floating homes, which are up to three storeys high and ninety-four feet long and sometimes outfitted with essentials like air conditioning, hot tubs, large-screen TVs, hardwood floors and granite countertops.

Houseboaters seeking solitude generally head north into Anstey Arm, nestled among abrupt, forested hillsides that sweep upward on the east side to the peaks of the Monashee Mountains. Anstey's upper end cannot be reached by road, and its lower end, at the middle of the H, can be reached only via a rough, washboardy logging road that takes an hour to travel from the nearest town, Sicamous, and only accesses the private lakefront properties that occupy some of the shoreline. Except for a few beaching spots that can host houseboats for the night, most of the remaining shoreline is rocky and uninhabited except for wildlife and, for a brief period, the Bushman.

I had the good fortune to spend some time on the Shuswap as a teenager and into my early twenties, when my family had a cabin on Salmon Arm, the southeast arm of the lake. Our slice of lake life provided plenty to occupy us, so there was little justification to spend a full day in a boat touring all the way up Anstey Arm. That changed, however, when I learned that the Bushman's cave had been discovered there. The prospect of seeing it was reason enough to explore the arm, and so on a sun-soaked summer day in 2002, I set out with some similarly curious friends for a visit.

Roughly halfway up the arm, past all the cabins, we saw a cluster of boats moored along a particularly forbidding section of shoreline. There was no obvious attraction there, so we wondered if perhaps we had stumbled upon some other cave seekers. We moored our boat against the serrated shoreline and found the switchback trail leading up the slope. It was tricky to navigate in flip flops, but it wasn't long before the doorway to the cave appeared abruptly in front of us.

Beyond the wood-framed entrance was an impactful glimpse into the Bushman's life. Even though the police had cleared out many of the contents, it felt like we were encroaching upon someone's home. It had a sensible arrangement, with enough space in the kitchen to comfortably prepare and enjoy a meal, and the bedroom chamber felt like it was located deep enough in the earth to safely ride out Armageddon. The custom-built framing and furniture suggested the Bushman had kept busy and was prepared to stay awhile. The reading material lying about suggested he enjoyed some leisure time—notwithstanding that the newspaper on the bed, folded over to reveal the picture of Osama bin Laden, felt slightly ominous in that setting. Putting that and the mildewy aroma aside, it was possible to see some attraction in the den as a short-term hideaway.

It was also possible to see how living there day to day might lead to anti-social tendencies or exacerbate any pre-existing ones.

Over the years since I set foot in his lair, I have continued to marvel at the effort required to construct it, and questions have percolated about its bearded occupant's motivation. He didn't seem to fit the profile of a refuge-seeking hermit who had drifted onto a wayward path or a freeloading, curmudgeonly misanthrope who had always been askew. There seemed to be more to him.

Curiosity kept pulling me in, and I began digging deeper and deeper. At some point, that curiosity morphed into a determination to answer the question of what had driven him to the cave. If nobody else was going to tell the full story, perhaps it would have to be me.

Margaret Atwood is partly responsible. While pondering the Bushman's story, I stumbled upon her 1972 book *Survival: A Thematic Guide to Canadian Literature*, which identified survival as the central symbol in Canadian literature. Her take on "survival" is broader than just fending off menacing elements in the bush: "In earlier writers these obstacles are external—the land, the climate, and so forth. In later writers the obstacles tend to become both harder to identify and more internal; they are no longer obstacles to physical survival but obstacles to what we may call spiritual survival, to life as anything more than a minimally human being. Sometimes fear of these obstacles becomes itself the obstacle, and a character is paralyzed by terror (either of what he thinks is threatening him from the outside, or of elements in his own nature that threaten him from within)."

As I learned more about the Bushman, his story seemed to hold the possibility of confronting most, if not all, of the obstacles to survival that the enduring author described a half century ago. Thus, with the prospect of unravelling a quintessential narrative—for vintage Canadian literature, at least—I sought to understand how someone ends up living in a cave in the bush. Or, as Atwood would say, into the darkness, looking for light, we go.

The Bushman's real name was John Bjornstrom, and the most recent address I could find for him was in the city of Williams Lake, a few hundred kilometres north of the Shuswap. I mailed letters to addresses I found for him there, tried various phone numbers and sent emails. No response came.

I had seen a comment from a user called "Shuswap Bushman" on an online message board dedicated to living off the grid that I had previously stumbled upon while doing some unrelated research on anchors. In response to a post on how to make your own anchor, the Bushman had offered a helpful modification. I revisited the site to see if I could retrieve any further information on his whereabouts, but his location was shown only as "Lake in the Woods," and the most recent reference to "Shuswap Bushman" on the forum was from another poster, calling himself The Hermit:

> I know it's been over 2 years and things change in life. I was never one of the stronger, most replying members in this forum, but this site/forum has always been a part of me since I signed in. The folks on this site are amazing. Polite, courteous, gracious and very helpful

people. Over the years you gain and lose members, some come and go, faster than they came. Some are like a legacy and gone—Shuswap Bushman. That is the joy of the Internet, we have our space to explore and learn, learn from other people's experiences and mistakes. Sad but part of life, we lose people in life, in our lives and on this forum.

But trawling online message boards didn't feel like the optimal approach for tracking down a man known as the Bushman. That is, until I stumbled upon a Kijiji ad offering documents for sale that, rather serendipitously, were being marketed to anyone interested in writing a book on the Bushman. The seller was a retired private investigator and friend of Bjornstrom's named Rob Nicholson, and the documents included a transcript of an interview with the Royal Canadian Mounted Police (RCMP) and correspondence from Bjornstrom. Nicholson explained that he had completed some investigative work to assist with Bjornstrom's trial preparation, which led to a friendship and the handing over of the documents for safekeeping; he had rediscovered them while in the process of moving. I purchased them for one hundred dollars plus postage. (I later learned from a *Salmon Arm Observer* article that a documentary crew had previously offered $5,000 for these same papers when the story "was still hot in the media," as Nicholson put it.)

When I initially contacted Nicholson and indicated I was exploring the prospect of a book, he said Bjornstrom hadn't written a book himself or sold the documents because he was not allowed to profit from his crimes. This was before British Columbia passed legislation in 2016 preventing criminals from profiting from their crimes—after convicted serial killer Robert Pickton proclaimed his innocence in a 144-page book that he authored, had smuggled out of prison, and then had published under a different name and made available on Amazon—but Bjornstrom, at the time of his sentencing, was given a specific court order to make sure he didn't sell his story in any fashion.

Nicholson volunteered to put me in touch with Bjornstrom, who he speculated was panning for gold in northern BC and might be unreachable for a while. He also cryptically warned that if I decided to write the book, I should be wary of potential "security concerns," but he didn't elaborate further. I wondered how I would explain that to my wife, but concluded that, for the time being, I could ignore the vague and presumably stale security threat.

I pursued a couple of other individuals with connections to Bjornstrom—they were also unsure of his whereabouts—but otherwise left it largely with Nicholson to make contact. A year later, when that had not happened, I concluded the next step was a road trip to Williams Lake to track him down in person. There was only one problem: on January 13, 2018, John Bjornstrom passed away from natural causes at the age of fifty-eight.

CHAPTER 3

THE CALL OF THE BUSH

❝ The bush is neutral. It is neither for nor against me . . . It is incapable of doing me harm."
Mors Kochanski, *Bushcraft: Outdoor Skills and Wilderness Survival*

Having been informed from media reports that Bjornstrom had been closest to his youngest sister, Jennifer, I went in search of her, and fortunately she was much easier to track down than Bjornstrom himself. She had a Facebook account, so I joined for the first time. (I later learned that even the Bushman had a Facebook account, the possibility of which I had failed to consider.) Within hours of messaging Jennifer, my phone rang. She was understandably apprehensive and skeptical of my intentions but ultimately agreed to meet me for lunch at Denny's in downtown Williams Lake. When she appeared there with a white cane, I apologized for causing her to travel to meet me. She explained she is visually impaired but still able to read large print on a computer screen and navigate familiar routes through town via a combination of buses and walking. We spent some time talking about the fire that had nearly engulfed the city a year earlier, forcing her to evacuate for sixteen days, but revisiting the experience still left her visibly shaken. Eventually our conversation turned to her brother, and she shed some light on his unordinary life.

John Bjornstrom began life as Nicholas Korody in Toronto in 1958. His birth parents, Nicholas Korody Sr. and Margaret Gizzella, were among the refugees who fled the post–World War II Soviet satellite state of Hungary following the Uprising of 1956. Many of them, including the Korodys, were Roma, often referred to as gypsies. They were stereotyped based largely on the work they undertook, which was compatible with their transient way of life: livestock trading, animal training, blacksmithing, entertaining, fortune telling. Their common heritage traces back to India, but sometime by the fourteenth century they had arrived in Europe.

Formalized persecution began a couple of centuries later, when the first anti-Romani legislation was introduced in the present-day Czech Republic. Gradually more European countries introduced legislation expelling them and even executing those who didn't comply. Attacks on the Roma escalated dramatically during the Holocaust, known to the Roma as Porajmos, or "the Devouring," when it's estimated that between 250,000 and 1.5 million Roma were executed by the Nazis.

In 1956 the general unrest in Hungary under Soviet control erupted into an uprising that led to the collapse of the government; before the Soviets reasserted control, more than two hundred thousand Hungarians fled. Canada had not yet signed on to the 1951 United Nations Refugee Convention, but the government improvised, organizing immigration screening procedures and transportation. Within the year, over thirty-seven thousand Hungarians were welcomed to Canada, including many Roma.

The Korodys landed in Toronto, but their marriage didn't survive the exodus despite the Romani history of families prevailing through migrations. They were divorced when their son was just two, and custody was granted to his father, a truck driver. Shortly thereafter, he was badly injured in an accident that left him unable to look after the boy, who was sent to a home for children run by the Pentecostal Church. Margaret, just nineteen at the time, had moved to Vancouver, but she was now able to gain custody, and her son eventually joined her on the West Coast.

Most of the '56ers, as the Hungarian immigrants came to be known, adjusted well to their adopted land. Historians have attributed this partly to the compassion and hospitality that greeted them and have recognized their integration as the template for Canada's ongoing sponsored refugee programs. But immigration was not a success for all. Margaret settled with her son into Vancouver's Downtown Eastside, which by the 1950s had become rundown as the city centre migrated westward. Once-popular hotels were converted into single-room occupancy housing, and beer parlours and brothels replaced theatres and shops. The area wasn't yet the magnet for drug users it would become, but Margaret still succumbed to addiction. She often left her son on his own or with strangers in rat-infested places even though he was unable to communicate well in English. She became involved in drug trafficking across the US border and was arrested. "The last time I saw her I was six years old and she was in a hospital bed," Bjornstrom recounted in front of a courtroom, though he was unsure exactly where the encounter took place. "She gave me a chocolate bar and I threw it away."

He was taken into foster care, then placed with a Norwegian couple, Sverre and Joanna Bjornstrom, in the Vancouver suburb of Burnaby. In search of a better life, they had emigrated in the 1940s from the small town of Bardu, Norway, close to the Arctic Circle, and became foster parents when they learned they were unable to have biological children. Despite the initial language barrier, they quickly grew attached to the boy, formally adopted him and renamed him John. The family eventually grew to include a total of four adopted children.

Jennifer told me the Bjornstroms treated their children very well. Sverre worked as a carpenter while Joanna worked at various jobs, including one at a marshmallow factory, memories of which brought a smile to Jennifer's face as she reminisced. When they weren't working, they tried to spend as much time as possible in the outdoors with their children—camping, fishing and skiing. Sometimes they would go to work and leave the children on their own for the day at a nearby lake with a tent trailer. Bjornstrom preferred this to school: he was a hyperactive kid and happiest in the bush. He had a strong affection for animals and would bring home various creatures he encountered, including stray and sick ones. One day he brought home a bullfrog and placed it in a box with holes, and the family watched as the box bounced around the house. He was enrolled in Boy Scouts and soaked up everything it had to teach him about the outdoors.

Despite being well treated at home, Bjornstrom ran away when he was twelve. At nearby Pitt Lake he found a partially sunk discarded boat that he repaired and used to travel to a small island. He had a tent with him, and for a couple of weeks he fished and snared small game to keep himself fed. His parents eventually figured out where he was and visited him. After their second visit, he decided to return home.

Burnaby was not ideal for Joanna, who had become sick and feared that the air quality at the coast was a factor. Friends from Norway were living in Williams Lake and encouraged the Bjornstroms to join them. Located in the Cariboo country of central BC, Williams Lake had a population of about four thousand at the time. It was, and continues to be, well known for hosting the annual Williams Lake Stampede, "The Greatest Show on Dirt," which precedes the Calgary Stampede's "Greatest Outdoor Show on Earth" on the rodeo circuit.

The rural life was an adjustment for some of the Bjornstrom family, but they soon grew to love their new home. They moved into a single wide trailer and purchased two horses they used to explore nearby lakes. Sverre split his time between building a house for the family and working as a carpentry foreman in Prince George, a few hours' drive farther north. John was soon riding horses bareback in rodeos and going hunting with his adoptive father. Sverre, who had served in World War II, owned various firearms that he used for hunting, and once John was able to shoot a quarter off a fencepost nine times out of ten, he was given his own gun.

Despite the appeal of Williams Lake, John was only there for one year before he asked his parents' permission to leave school and find work. Around the same time, a neighbourhood girl had become pregnant, and Joanna believed her adopted son was responsible, which had created friction in the family. The girl later told Joanna that there had never been any intimacy between them, but by the time the misunderstanding was sorted out, Bjornstrom's parents had already warned him that if he wanted to work instead of completing school, he would have to leave home. So at the age of fourteen, before completing grade nine, he ventured off on his horse, Charlotte, and found work at the Alkali Lake Ranch south of Williams Lake.

After a summer working odd jobs on the ranch and sensing the limitations of his opportunities there, he set off across the mountains on horseback for Alberta. He didn't have trouble finding work on ranches, initially patrolling ranges, and one summer Jennifer was able to visit him for two weeks on a ranch near Camrose. Another of his jobs was at the Big Coulee Cattle Company farther south, where he eventually managed a large herd of Simmental cattle. He also got involved with farming operations—tilling, seeding and harvesting—and out of necessity became comfortable with repairing farm equipment.

In his twenties, enticed by the oil boom and the freedom of the road, Bjornstrom began driving long-haul trucks. Initially he hauled explosives used in seismic exploration to locate oil and gas reserves and other underground deposits, and some of his trips took him through Williams Lake to deliver explosives to a local mine, providing him with a convenient way to see his family. In the spring of 1980 he was living in an apartment in Grande Prairie, Alberta, when a family from Ontario moved in next door with a seventeen-year-old daughter who caught his eye. Her name was Lucette.

Lucette now lives in Kapuskasing, in northeastern Ontario, which is where I met up with her. The town was developed in the 1920s as a result of a partnership between the New York Times Company and the Kimberly-Clark Corporation to secure a stable wood supply from the surrounding sea of boreal forest for producing newsprint and Kleenex. Although the town is not particularly close to the Quebec border, French is the predominant language, as many workers migrated there from Quebec.

Lucette grew up here in a francophone family but like most people in the area is perfectly bilingual. Her father, a trucker, was enticed to Grande Prairie in 1980 by the booming Alberta economy and a job that was supposed to be waiting for him. After settling his family into an apartment next to Bjornstrom's, he struck up a conversation with the fellow trucker. "That young man would be good for you," he told his daughter afterwards. A few days later, Bjornstrom showed up at McDonald's, where Lucette was working, with a dozen red roses in hand. She agreed to a date with the "very good-looking cowboy." He taught her how to square dance and took her to see the country singer Barbara Mandrell.

Their courtship was soon tested when it became apparent that the job opportunities in Alberta were not as readily available as hoped. And despite its French name, Grande Prairie was an anglophone city, and Lucette's family found it difficult to fit in as francophones. It was a large convoy that made its way back across the country: Lucette's father led in his ten-wheeler, her mother drove the family van, her sister drove a pickup truck with a goat in the back that her mother had purchased on a whim, her brother-in-law drove his truck and Lucette joined

Bjornstrom in his truck with his horse, Charlotte, in a trailer behind it. Back in Ontario, the young couple settled in a small town called Opasatika, down the road from Kapuskasing. A couple of months later, Lucette was pregnant.

But just as Lucette's family had found it hard to fit into the anglophone culture of Grande Prairie, Bjornstrom found it difficult to adjust to the francophone environment, and his employment opportunities were limited. "My French is only enough to get me in trouble, but not enough to get me out of it," was how he described his fluency level. More inconveniently, however, he was due back in Alberta to serve out a jail sentence. According to Bjornstrom, before landing in Grande Prairie, he had been hauling cargo for a company out of Coronation, Alberta, with his own truck. When the company hadn't paid him for several months, he forged cheques on the company's account for what he was owed to cover his expenses, and "not a cent more." He was handed a six-month sentence for theft and forgery. He had neglected to inform Lucette of his impending incarceration, and being seven months pregnant when he left, she was forced to move back in with her parents.

She gave birth to a girl and named her Julie. Unsure if she could raise a child on her own, she put Julie up for adoption without telling her parents. When the local priest who managed the adoption process showed up to take Julie away, the grandparents intervened and committed to raising her themselves. Bjornstrom eventually returned and asked Lucette to take him back, but she feared a repeat vanishing act and rejected him.

Bjornstrom remained in the area and was able to see Julie regularly. He trained as a blacksmith and found work tending to horses' hooves to supplement his trucking income, and attended an agricultural college with ambitions of opening a riding stable. He became known to locals as Cowboy John after he returned to bareback riding in rodeos and tried his hand as a bullfighter (otherwise known as a rodeo protection athlete). He also found work as a guide for the Ontario Provincial Police, escorting officers through the backcountry and teaching them survival skills, including hunting. Eventually he started seeing another woman, and they had two children together, but she left with the kids for city life in southern Ontario when the children were young, and they remained largely estranged from him.

In 1989 Bjornstrom returned to Alberta. There, his search for work became entangled with a special ability he believed he possessed, which he thought could be of help to others: a sixth sense.

CHAPTER 4

STARGATE

> Fifty years of laboratory parapsychology experiments have demonstrated that many people can perceive information inaccessible to the 'conventional five senses' . . . a few individuals have so developed this process that they can provide detailed descriptions of hidden or concealed events, places, people, objects, feelings, and color with considerable consistency."
>
> From a 1986 report entitled "A Suggested Remote Viewing Training Procedure" released with numerous other previously declassified documents by the US government in 2017

The first confluence of Bjornstrom's career path and his psychic interests had occurred back in 1982, when he was hauling munitions from the Canadian Professional Munitions factory in Raymond, Alberta, to various military bases. At the Fairchild Air Force Base southwest of Spokane, Washington, he spotted a recruitment ad for individuals with psychic abilities. As a kid, Bjornstrom had become convinced he had a sixth sense that allowed him to foresee future events and acquire knowledge he had no natural means of acquiring. Eager to explore his psychic potential and intrigued by the ad's suggestion that a career awaited successful applicants, he applied and was invited to attend a screening event in Washington, DC.

His bus ticket paid for, he made his way to the US capital. Upon arriving there he was evaluated with other respondents at an office in a twelve-storey building near the White House. He made it through the initial screening and spent six weeks living in a government house with other participants before being transferred to the Philadelphia area for more testing at a building with a hospital-like atmosphere. The tests were designed to evaluate his remote viewing ability and typically entailed looking at a picture of something—a missing person, boat, submarine, plane—and then identifying its location on a map. "They'd have you plugged into all kinds of wires, probes or wires taped to your head and chest, and they'd watch you continuously," he later testified at his trial.

The program, eventually known as Stargate, was originated in the 1970s by the CIA in response to suspicions the Soviets were ramping up their spending on the use of extrasensory perception for espionage purposes. The Defense Intelligence Agency (DIA), which provides intelligence for combat-related missions, took over responsibility for the program in the 1980s. At the time of Bjornstrom's involvement, he said, the program was led by Colonel Harold E. Phillips. According to *Out There: The Government's Secret Quest for Extraterrestrials*, a book by former *New York Times* reporter Howard Blum, Phillips was a DIA intelligence analyst who had worked with remote viewers in the 1980s before going on to head up a UFO working group.

In 1995, for a special program called *Put to the Test*, ABC News interviewed Joseph McMoneagle, a retired army warrant officer who carried out remote viewing operations from within a leaky old wooden barracks at Fort Meade, Maryland, with roughly fifteen other remote viewers. A typical daily task was describing or drawing details about a person, place or thing of which they had no prior knowledge. According to McMoneagle, it was shown to work about 15 per cent of the time, which in his opinion was better than many other intelligence collection services.

The American Institutes for Research, a non-profit research organization tasked with evaluating the utility of remote viewing for the intelligence community, also found a statistically significant effect in their laboratory tests. Their findings were tempered by the lack of evidence supporting the "origins or nature of the phenomenon," but even more problematic was that the information collected was often found to be vague and ambiguous and lacked the requisite ingredients for actionable intelligence. That marked the end of the program.

I reviewed some of the declassified files from the Stargate program, which was itself an ethereal experience. Several documents contain information on the civilian recruitment efforts that had been ramped up in the 1980s. One of them lays out some of the characteristics attributable to successful remote viewers: "open-minded, adventurous, above average intelligence, mature and stable, 'artistic' in character and personality, successful, well thought of by self and co-workers, articulate, sensitive, and have an ability to 'in-flow' data." Consideration was also given to those with previous "psychoenergetic experience." Not to be considered, however, were occult fanatics, mystical zealots or those who displayed an unreasonable enthusiasm for psychoenergetics.

Most of the screening sessions were contracted out to a research company named SRI International. Participants were recruited through advertisements for a remote viewing seminar; attendees were invited to recruitment trials in Washington, DC, and San Francisco. The Washington location was just across the Potomac River from the White House, which is consistent with Bjornstrom's description of his first posting. (The declassified files refer to psychoenergetics research at other facilities, including St. Joseph's University, which is located in suburban Philadelphia and presumably the other location where Bjornstrom spent time remote viewing.)

Screening was a two-stage process to whittle participants down from several hundred to five to ten individuals who demonstrated "robust RV [remote viewing] performance." The sessions began with a lecture presentation, and then participants were instructed to relax, take a few deep breaths and try to focus on the task to be presented. Meanwhile, in another room, an assistant was waiting to begin communicating telepathically. Upon receiving the signal to start—a single ring of the telephone—the assistant opened an envelope and began viewing the corresponding material on a television monitor. The material, selected from sixteen random target videos, varied widely: James Bond skiing off a cliff in *The Spy Who Loved Me*; ostriches performing a synchronized dance; a clip from *Superman IV* in which a jolly cosmonaut does repair work outside a space station while singing "My Way" in Russian, only to be knocked into space by an errant satellite and rescued by Superman, who puts him back in the space station and tells him in Russian, "You'll be safer singing in here."

While the telepathic sender continually viewed the target video, participants drew or wrote down their perceptions on forms. Those who identified more elements than could be attributable to chance alone were asked to continue. In the second-stage screening the same targets were used but there was no sender—participants were now expected to identify target material that nobody was looking at, as if receiving telepathic signals wasn't enough. Those who succeeded were deemed to have demonstrated robust RV.

When I asked Rob Nicholson—the former private investigator who sold me the Bushman documents—what he made of all this, he said he had previously worked with an intelligence operative in the US and had asked her about Bjornstrom. Her response was that he had made it through the screening process and was a good "farmer," a euphemism for "trainee" that had originated at the main intelligence training grounds in Williamsburg, Virginia, which was also known as the Farm. However, despite Bjornstrom having some alleged success in the program, the experience left him unsettled and battling nightmares, so he left. He walked away from the Philadelphia facility and caught a bus back to Canada.

Nonetheless, if this experience gave Bjornstrom some validation of his sixth sense, it would help to explain what happened in the early 1990s, after he returned to Alberta—starting with his decision to establish a private investigation business. Up to that point, most of his work experience had consisted of driving trucks, managing cattle and farriering, so launching a new business as a private investigator was a curious career move. But perhaps the Stargate program had given him the confidence to believe he had a valuable service to offer. After taking some investigative and police science courses by correspondence, he rented an office in a building in an industrial park in southeast Calgary, where he headquartered his new venture, which he named Sir Pegasus. The company was listed with the Better Business Bureau from 1995 to 1998.

His investigative work included completing background checks on potential employees for companies, spying on cheating spouses and looking for missing children. He took on other, more routine jobs as well, such as monitoring traffic flows for potential restaurant locations and helping people find work. Things were soon going well for his new company, and he was talking regularly to Julie and Lucette. Lucette had married another man, with whom she had two more children, but her husband had recently passed away. That led to her reconnecting with Bjornstrom, who had quickly developed a relationship with her new children, and she began talking about joining him in Calgary.

It was around that time that Bjornstrom took on a local client named David Walsh, the president of a soon-to-be infamous company named Bre-X, which held a majority stake in a potential Indonesian gold mine. Bjornstrom had been having a drink in a downtown Calgary lounge with a friend when Walsh entered the lounge, also with a friend. The two friends knew each other, and the four men ended up having a beer together. A few days later, Bjornstrom received a call from Walsh asking if he could help him out with some investigative work. Bjornstrom agreed and was given some money up front.

Bre-X was no ordinary company and had more need for investigators than most, but Bjornstrom likely wouldn't have appreciated just how much of an imbroglio Walsh found himself in. Undoubtedly there are many people who wish they had never become embroiled in the cautionary tale. Most entanglements were limited to financial losses. According to Bjornstrom, his own involvement landed him on a hit list.

SOUTHEAST ASIA

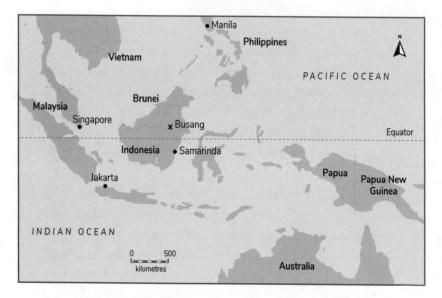

CHAPTER 5

GILDED DREAMS

> Somewhere in the cell-structure of the brain, is located an organ which receives vibrations of thought ordinarily called 'hunches.' So far, science has not discovered where this organ of the sixth sense is located, but this is not important. The fact remains that human beings do receive accurate knowledge, through sources other than the physical senses. Such knowledge, generally, is received when the mind is under the influence of extraordinary stimulation. Any emergency which arouses the emotions, and causes the heart to beat more rapidly than normal may, and generally does, bring the sixth sense into action."

Napoleon Hill, *Think and Grow Rich*

David Walsh was raised in the wealthy Westmount neighbourhood of Montreal and, like Bjornstrom, was a high school dropout. He followed his father and grandfather into stockbroking, a field in which a lack of a formal education was not an impediment at the time. At seventeen he was buying and selling stocks and bonds on behalf of wealthy individuals and pension funds. By the time he was twenty-three, he was the head of a three-person team and had charmed a secretary named Jeannette into marrying him. They had two sons shortly thereafter.

Walsh's philosophy on amassing wealth was inspired by a self-improvement book called *Think and Grow Rich*, by Napoleon Hill, which was published during the Great Depression and has now sold over 100 million copies, according to the Napoleon Hill Foundation. After mastering all the other principles described in the book, the author claimed, readers might be able to access that portion of the subconscious mind that receives ideas and knowledge as a flash into the mind—the sixth sense. He goes on to describe it as a subject that "will be of great interest and benefit to the person whose aim is to accumulate vast wealth." Walsh claimed to have read the book at least fifty times after it was passed along to him by his mother, who had received it from her mother.

Walsh's first attempt at striking out on his own came after the company he was working for alleged he had failed to detect fraudulent transactions connected to one of the accounts he was supervising. He left the company and launched his own trust company, and when it quickly flopped, he joined a larger investment dealer, where his schmoozing abilities generated decent commissions on the sales desk. In 1982 he was asked to set up an institutional trading desk in Calgary, an enticing move since Calgary had been flourishing as a home for the companies benefiting from the same oil and gas boom that had drawn Lucette's family west.

His timing couldn't have been worse. The recession of the early 1980s was just beginning. Unemployment reached 12 per cent, and house prices plunged by more than 20 per cent. These strong headwinds imperiled Walsh's new venture, and he abandoned it just a year later.

Increasingly desperate for a success, he spent the rest of the 1980s starting up unsuccessful oil, gas and mineral exploration companies—when he wasn't sitting in Moose McGuire's or the Three Greenhorns with other promoters, sucking back drinks and cigarettes. The Walsh family kept afloat on Jeannette's income as a secretary and Walsh's stock-flipping and lines of credit. He moved his office into the basement of the family home. Eventually the continual rolling of the dice caught up to him—he was overextended to fifteen credit card companies—and in 1992 he declared bankruptcy.

Undeterred, Walsh opted to roll the dice one more time. Bre-X Minerals Ltd., a mineral exploration company he had started up and named after his son, Brett, was still trading for pennies on the Alberta Stock Exchange, and Walsh somehow managed to raise some money to breathe new life into it. He then set off for Indonesia to look for the next big opportunity— an idea, he said, that came to him in a dream.

The only person he knew in Indonesia was a Dutch geologist named John Felderhof, an intrepid mineral prospector who relished mucking about in inhospitable jungles in search of the big prize. Raised in the Netherlands and then, from the age of fourteen, in Nova Scotia, Felderhof studied geology at Dalhousie University in Halifax and then left for Northern Rhodesia (now Zambia), where he worked in a copper mine, married a South

African and began raising a family with her until safety concerns and international sanctions caused him to leave.

Felderhof's next opportunity landed the family in Papua New Guinea, where he and another geologist hacked their way through the dense bush with machetes and stumbled upon communities untouched by modern civilization. On one occasion when Felderhof lost his sodden boots while hiking through a waist-deep swamp, he continued barefoot and afterwards had to remove eighteen leeches from his legs with a lit cigarette. The persistence of the two men culminated in the discovery of a massive copper and gold deposit, which would result in the construction of the Ok Tedi Mine nearly twenty years later. This gained Felderhof notoriety as a geologist, but it did not bring him the financial windfall he sought, as he didn't own a stake in the project.

By 1970, too many rounds with malaria had tempered his enthusiasm for Papua New Guinea, and he tried to repeat his success, with a greater financial stake, throughout Africa, Australia and Asia. The lifestyle eventually became too much for his marriage, which ended in divorce after seventeen years. Several years later, he met an Australian woman named Ingrid who left her husband, married Felderhof and bought a house in Australia with him.

In 1980 Felderhof landed in Indonesia, renting motorbikes to travel from village to village seeking out locals who had found gold nuggets in stream beds. One area that kindled his interest was around Busang Creek on the island of Kalimantan, but he concluded it was too remote and expensive to explore. By the early 1990s he was broke and out of work and had developed a reputation for exaggeration and binge drinking. Meanwhile,

Ingrid had moved in with his family in Nova Scotia to weather the storm.

It was under these circumstances that David Walsh reached out to him in 1993. The two men had much in common at that point; both were penniless, heavy-drinking, chain-smoking speculators determined to find something, even if it meant going through hell first. They met at the Sari Pan Pacific, a ritzy hotel in Jakarta. Walsh was accompanied by his son Sean—a recent high school graduate possibly brought along because his credit card wasn't frozen—and a geologist who had worked with Walsh previously. Felderhof was accompanied by a few geologists, including a Filipino he had mentored named Michael de Guzman. Over dinner they reviewed a portfolio of properties Felderhof had compiled.

Walsh decided Busang was the most attractive property Felderhof had presented to him, partly because the report compiled by de Guzman generously estimated the resource there at 1.3 million ounces of mineable gold. Felderhof was brought on as Bre-X's Indonesian manager, and he in turn hired de Guzman as his chief geologist. To raise money to develop the project, Walsh and Felderhof paraded their prospect through the offices of potential investors across Canada. Thanks to an improving market for junior mining companies in the early 1990s following the market crash of 1987, they were able to raise enough money to acquire the property and begin testing it, albeit on a shoestring budget.

Work began in 1993 in the central zone with the assembled team of geologists overseeing local workers. Bulldozers were used to carve rough roads through the jungle, followed by trucks towing thirty-foot drill rigs. Drilling commenced with the sacrifice of a chicken to placate the local tribe's gods, and then diamond-studded bits were sunk up to 1,300 feet into the bedrock. Hollow pipe encapsulated core samples that, once extracted, were broken into shorter lengths with sledgehammers, washed, loaded into wooden crates and transported back to the base camp by truck. At the camp the samples were logged and partly crushed to prepare them for further transport downstream by boat to a laboratory for assaying.

The assay results for the first two holes were not encouraging, and Felderhof gave instructions to shut down the operation, but before that happened, a third hole was drilled that showed more promise. The operation continued. Results improved dramatically for holes four through nine, which showed an attractive range of eight to sixteen grams per tonne.

The company's prospects now changed dramatically. They worked the phones and raised funds to acquire a 90 per cent interest in adjacent lands to the southeast, reserving the other 10 per cent for the required local ownership. They convinced the retiring head of exploration at Barrick Gold, Paul Kavanagh, to visit the property. He liked what he saw and was persuaded to join the Bre-X board of directors, providing instant credibility, and a $4.5 million equity raise was completed in 1994 at $1.50 per share.

When drilling expanded into the southeast zone, even more fruitful results were encountered. Some of the gold was found near the surface, making it easier to extract. The drilling gathered more pace throughout 1995, as step-out drilling locations were all encountering gold, further delineating the massive size of the deposit and causing the resource estimate to balloon. "A resource of 30 million ounces can be readily attained,"

Felderhof announced in January 1996. That would make it the fourth-largest gold deposit discovered anywhere in the world.

By then many of the investment newsletter authors and equity research analysts had developed gold fever, and several visited the site, returning to write ever more enthusiastic reports with higher and higher price targets. One such report advised readers that "the foremost and primary rule of investing in the junior resource industry is to have confidence in the people behind the company," and it suggested that such was the case with David Walsh, "one of the sharpest executive officers that we have ever encountered in this business. He is also one of the most honest and dependable."

When the author of that report was interviewed by *Fools' Gold* author Brian Hutchinson, he could no longer remember why he had given Walsh such glowing praise. He had never actually met the man—nor anyone else from Bre-X, for that matter—and had only spoken to Walsh on the phone. His actual assessment, which he withheld from his readers, was that Walsh was the "weak link" and that he had a drinking problem. Meanwhile, the report's author had bought Bre-X at $1.20 and sold at $250.

In May 1996 the stock price reached $286.50 (on a pre-split basis), giving the company a sky-high valuation of over $6 billion. Felderhof sold $19 million in shares that month alone and purchased an ocean-front house and condominium in the Grand Caymans, a house in the US and a Lamborghini. He would sell $84 million in total over the span of about four months, according to the Ontario Securities Commission. Walsh, who had only just moved out of his basement office to half-completed Bre-X offices in a downtown Calgary building, had begun selling shares earlier than Felderhof and would divest $56 million of Bre-X shares in total, including those belonging to his wife. The couple opted for one property in the Bahamas, where they would soon take refuge.

CHAPTER 6

GILDED GREED

> I did not know that mankind were suffering for want of gold. I
> have seen a little of it. I know that it is very malleable, but not so
> malleable as wit. A grain of gold will gild a great surface, but not
> so much as a grain of wisdom."
> **Henry Thoreau,** "Life Without Principle"

Transparency International, a corruption-fighting non-governmental organization, launched its first International Corruption Index in 1995, around the same time the Bre-X management team was declaring they had made one of the world's pre-eminent gold discoveries. The inaugural index ranked Indonesia the most corrupt of forty-one countries surveyed. It also conferred the title of most corrupt leader in modern history upon Suharto, the president of Indonesia from 1967 to 1998. His tyrannical rule left hundreds of thousands dead, and he is alleged to have embezzled between US$15 billion and US$35 billion from the state.

Few sectors of the economy were left untapped by the Suharto family. When it came to natural resources, a common approach was for a related party—often one of Suharto's six children—to act as a conduit around any bureaucratic hurdles. In exchange, the related party usually ended up with a meaningful stake in the business or lucrative contracts for providing services to the venture. When Jakarta's water system was privatized, Suharto's son Sigit ended up with a 20 per cent stake in the winning bidder. The state oil company, Pertamina, had roughly 170 contracts with omnipresent Suharto family businesses providing everything from cafeteria food to security. When the company was audited in 1999, over US$6 billion was estimated to have been lost due to corruption and other inefficiencies.

As no foreigners were allowed mining permits in Indonesia without Suharto's authorization, the Bre-X management team knew they were not going to lay claim to billions of dollars' worth of Indonesian gold without Suharto's family taking a cut. That was also apparent to Peter Munk, the Hungarian-born Canadian businessman who had founded Barrick Gold in 1983 and grown it into one of the world's largest mining companies. In 1993 he had been rebuffed in an attempt to acquire Bre-X, but he was not going to let it get away a second time. So while the Bre-X management was busy pumping the share price up and selling off their shares, Munk was arduously pursuing any angle he could find to take control of the Busang prospect.

One of Munk's tactics was to woo the eldest of Suharto's children, a daughter known as Tutut, who was regarded as having the most economic and political clout of Suharto's offspring. She was persuaded to help expedite Barrick's position in exchange for one of her companies being granted the right to build some of the mine's infrastructure. (A Barrick employee later described partnering with the Suharto family as follows: "You can never control your destiny once you're in bed with the Suharto children. They demand money, and then they want more. They say give me this and give me that, and it never ends. You can never budget anything, never control anything. You're on the ropes the whole time.")

Munk also used some of his illustrious connections to apply pressure on the Indonesian government. Brian Mulroney and George H.W. Bush, both looking for new pursuits after holding the highest offices of their respective countries, were part of the Barrick offensive and sat on an international advisory board created to guide the company through "geopolitical tangles." Both wrote letters to the Indonesian government suggesting the company should be given the opportunity to develop the Busang site.

An American investigative firm was also hired by Barrick to unearth weaknesses in Bre-X's position, and they came back with several exploitable instances of Bre-X operating outside the Indonesian government's rules, including the lack of proper title to the property. When the Bre-X team tried to renew their exploration permit, it was cancelled owing to some vague "administrative problems." Although the news shaved roughly half a billion from Bre-X's market capitalization, it was relatively minor damage for the company at the time and only indicated the market believed they would find a solution.

Walsh was indeed desperate for a way to break through the impasse. He had long been irked by the arrogance and under-handedness of Barrick's approach—including Munk's peculiar practice of referring to him as "darling"—and he sought to counter with his own strategic alliance. In October Bre-X announced it had become aligned with a private Indonesian company controlled by the second eldest of Suharto's children, Sigit. It was a startling move to most people familiar with the country's inner workings, as Sigit was known more for being a serial gambler than for business or political acumen.

The arrangement did little to counter Barrick's finagling, and Bre-X was blindsided a month later when the Indonesian government gave the company "guidance" to form a partnership with Barrick, in which Barrick was to get a 75 per cent interest and Bre-X the remaining 25 per cent. For brokering the deal, "the Indonesian government would appreciate it if the parties could consider a 10 per cent participation given to the Indonesian government." Barrick and Bre-X would have to agree on a purchase price.

At the time, many of Indonesia's civil servants who had overseen the development of a fair and transparent regulatory system for mining were struggling with the growing publicity surrounding their government's machinations. One technocrat, who was on the verge of tears while speaking with journalist Brian Hutchinson, commented that "three decades of solid mining law had been undermined in a matter of weeks, thanks to a handful of local politicians and some shortsighted Canadian businessmen." The deal with Barrick wasn't a given, however, as other powerbrokers and courtiers had begun putting pressure on the Indonesian government to consider an auction process for the Busang property.

Sigit, the Suharto offspring whom Bre-X had gambled on, was also becoming concerned that his sister's arrangement with Barrick was going to rob him of a lucrative deal, and he turned to his father's long-time crony, Mohamad "Bob" Hasan, to intervene. Hasan and Suharto met when Suharto was a junior army officer and Hasan supplied provisions to the army. Hasan is rumored to have assisted Suharto with a smuggling operation, and he helped him cultivate relationships with senior officers in Jakarta, which proved valuable when Suharto's forces overthrew the government in the 1960s. Suharto rewarded Hasan with valuable concessions, which he parlayed into holdings in other industries. The two had a weekly tee time at which they discussed their joint interests, often in the company of dignitaries and celebrities. After a round with Sylvester Stallone, Hasan boasted: "I told Rambo, 'I'm the king of the jungle.'"

He also took on the role of mediator among Suharto's children following the death of Suharto's wife in 1996, earning him the moniker "Uncle Bob." He had just recently settled a dispute between two of them, known as Tommy and Bambang, over ownership of an auto manufacturer that produced the Timor "national car," a vehicle that nobody in the country liked but consumers still bought because of its special exemptions from duties, luxury taxes and tariffs on imported spare parts.

When Hasan took a closer look at Busang, his self-interest was piqued. Over a round of golf, he convinced Suharto to allow him to broker a deal. A company he controlled quietly acquired a 50 per cent interest in Bre-X's minority Indonesian partner in the main zone, a valuable position given that the partner held the mining authorization, which was only available to Indonesian companies. Sigit was given a 10 per cent interest in the Hasan-controlled company, presumably for bringing the opportunity to Uncle Bob's attention. Tutut, who was working on behalf of Barrick, was excluded.

By this point, Barrick was not the only company pursuing Bre-X. However, none of the others vying for control of the Busang property had the relationship with Hasan that James "Jim Bob" Moffett had as chairman of Freeport-McMoRan Copper & Gold, a company based in the US that operated the Grasberg gold mine in Indonesia. Moffett had been assiduously courting Suharto and his cronies for years, paying for vacations and college educations for some of their children and bringing them in on deals. A Hasan-controlled company had even acquired a minority stake in Freeport thanks to Freeport backstopping a loan and lending Hasan funds to cover the interest.

While the tangled process of determining an equitable ownership structure of Busang was underway, negative publicity suddenly emerged about Freeport's competitors. Munk's past business failures were publicized (mingled with anti-Semitic references to his Jewish faith), and the financial position and environmental record of others was questioned. Freeport was spared similar attention, even though insurance held by the company had recently been revoked because of environmental concerns at the Grasberg Mine.

With the playing field sufficiently tilted, Hasan settled the ownership of Busang in February 1997, and Freeport was awarded—or burdened, depending on perspective—with an ownership stake. Bre-X would retain a 45 per cent interest, the Indonesian government would receive 10 per cent and Freeport would get 15 per cent while financing 25 per cent of the mine's cost. The remaining 30 per cent would go to two companies now controlled by the éminence grise himself, Uncle Bob.

Although blindsided, Walsh tried to reassure the market that it was a fair deal.

Felderhof argued that they were in the government's sights because they had discovered "too much gold, so it therefore becomes a question of national interest." On a call with research analysts Felderhof said that being reduced to a 45 per cent stake wasn't a big deal: "We are dealing with a very unusual deposit here, and it's one of a kind in the world. Once we finish the drilling program we are currently doing . . . my estimate is 95 million ounces. Mike de Guzman, my project manager, he estimates 100 million ounces. If you would ask me what is the total potential, I would feel very comfortable with 200 million ounces. So far as I am concerned, there's lots of blue sky there."

Now that Freeport was a reluctant partner in Busang, they set about trying to confirm that gold had indeed been found there. Based on their extensive experience in Indonesia, much of it around their Grasberg mine, they were understandably skeptical. They had been turning over rocks in the area for half a century and had amassed total gold reserves of 52 million ounces. They were, therefore, having difficulty reconciling that with Bre-X's estimate of a 200-million-ounce deposit discovered over such a short time span, a claim that hadn't been independently verified. Their doubts were reinforced when their geologists reached the site to begin testing.

Bre-X had claimed that, based on their drilling results, the gold deposit was present right to the surface. If so, Freeport's geologists expected to find signs of panning by the local Dayak people, but suspiciously, none were encountered. Freeport's geologists took samples from exposed features while preparing to drill their initial test holes, and they quickly determined there were no signs of gold at the surface. (The Bre-X geologists would later be questioned about the absence of gold in outcrop samples, and their explanations included that it had leached, evaporated or "gone somewhere.") Results from seven test holes showed no more gold than what is typically found in seawater. In contrast, assay results from drilling samples stored at a Bre-X warehouse in Samarinda contained more gold, albeit uncommonly large grains with a high content of silver in the centre—the kind of gold typically found in the Dayaks' alluvial washings, not the igneous gold they would encounter in bedrock.

Moffett decided he should convey the concerning findings to Walsh. Members of the Prospectors & Developers Association of Canada (PDAC) had assembled in Toronto for their annual convention, regarded as the "premier international event" of the mineral industry. The Bre-X senior management, including all the senior geologists from Indonesia, were there to watch Felderhof receive the Prospector of the Year award. Eventually Moffet was able to get Walsh on the phone: "David, we've got a problem." Walsh replied that he was a financial person and Felderhof was the one to speak with. Felderhof countered that Freeport had surely made a mistake, but they would send someone to the site to help rectify the problem. After some discussion it was decided that de Guzman would meet with Freeport to sort it out.

"We waited and waited and waited," Moffett said, "and he never arrived."

CHAPTER 7

THE SORCERER

> ❝ And now, the end is near
> And so I face the final curtain . . ."
> "My Way," words by **Paul Anka**

When Michael de Guzman was young, a random attack by a gang of thugs shattered his knee along with his dreams of playing for the Philippines national basketball team and left him with a pronounced limp for the rest of his life. Aside from that and perhaps his wispy mustache, it would be hard to distinguish him in a crowd. Shrouded behind his inconspicuous outward appearance, however, was a confounding web of entanglement.

Not only would de Guzman be accused of orchestrating one of the most elaborate mining frauds of all time, but he also had an abnormal penchant for marriage. In all, he was married to four women at the same time—making him a quadragamist, the top end of polygamy classifications—and none of them was aware of the others. In Indonesia, the law allows men to enter into marriage with up to four women simultaneously, but that same law specifies that each newcomer to the marriage must receive the blessing of the existing wives by way of consent letters, and the husband must provide evidence that he can support all his wives and treat them equally.

In de Guzman's native Philippines polygamy is permitted only for Muslims, which de Guzman was not, or at least not when he married his first wife, Teresa, in a Catholic ceremony. He had recently completed a master's degree in geology from a university in Manila, the city in which he had been raised with his eleven siblings (coincidentally, he and Felderhof were both the fifth of twelve children). Upon graduating he was given a job as a geology trainee by the Benguet Corporation at their Acupan mine, and the newlywed couple moved into a fully furnished, three-bedroom home to start raising a family. De Guzman divided most of his time between work, family and church, though he was known to occasionally unwind at one of the "gentlemen's clubs" or karaoke bars down the mountain road in the town of Baguio.

He enjoyed the detailed geological work of mapping, sampling and core-logging, but he also honed his presentation skills, taking a Dale Carnegie course to improve his public speaking ability and overall confidence. "He had exceptional talent," recalled Birl Worley, his American-born boss and de Guzman's apparent role model for exerting confidence. "He had a marvelous mind and saw things that even I failed to see, and I thought I was probably one of the best observers and recorders that God put on the face of the earth." In time he became Acupan's chief geologist.

With greater responsibility, his enthusiasm for the job waned because much of his work now involved supervising miners as opposed to the exploratory work for the geological prizes he coveted. According to Worley, he was also mistreated for not going along with corrupt middle managers involved in a gold theft ring. So in 1987, when an Australian geologist visited the Philippines to enlist a team to join the burgeoning gold rush in Indonesia, de Guzman jumped at the opportunity. He took with him a geologist he had been working with at Acupan named Cesar Puspos, who, according to Worley, was a very honest and professional employee. Awaiting them in Indonesia was their new boss, John Felderhof.

De Guzman undertook the exploration responsibilities at a prospect called Mirah, but after meagre results it was ordered to be put on hold. His interpretation of the assay results left him less inclined to abandon the project, however, and he ordered the drilling of a rogue hole, which identified enough gold to keep the project alive, albeit barely. (After numerous hiccups the Mirah project was eventually commissioned in 2012.) Shortly thereafter, he married his second wife, SuGenie, or Genie as he called her. The two lived together while he worked on another project that was shortly abandoned.

The prospects for the mining industry deteriorated at the end of the 1980s and the three geologists began jumping from job to job, ever more desperate. De Guzman and Puspos worked on a gold project in Java, but that lasted only a year. De Guzman's boss there described him as "a workaholic and sometimes too optimistic about the resources, but he was honest. I had no problems with Mike." Others described him as being invaluable and a "geological guru." He was given the nickname "Sorcerer" for his ability to combine his pervasive geological knowledge with his persuasive presentation skills.

In 1992, when Felderhof was hired to investigate the Busang prospect, it was de Guzman he sent into the bush to have a closer look. De Guzman hiked for over thirty kilometres and investigated the site for four days while collecting samples (and reputedly encountering headhunters). He compared the geological setting to Acupan back in the Philippines and extrapolated a generous resource estimate based on the limited information available. That report would become the basis for Bre-X's decision to focus on Busang after the fateful meeting at the Sari Pan Pacific in Jakarta a few months later.

When the Bre-X drilling program kicked off, de Guzman was tasked with overseeing it, and subsequent reports show that salting of the samples with traces of gold must have begun with the third hole, which was crudely salted with a man-made copper-gold alloy, possibly from a piece of jewelry. It is estimated that during the next three years over twenty-five thousand samples were salted, though in a much more sophisticated fashion. Many questions remain, including who was involved in the salting and the origin of the salted gold. Crew members on site included surveyors, two samplers, an eight-man drill crew and camp labourers.

One of the samplers, a metallurgist named Jerome Alo who had worked with de Guzman and Puspos in the Philippines, was brought on after the third hole to oversee the sample preparation on site, even though metallurgists typically work at operating mines or in laboratories. Birl Worley told The Northern Miner, the industry's journal of record, that he did not hold Alo in high regard, based on his experience with him in the Philippines: "Alo was inside the mill and he was making the figures up, so I got rid of him. Some of the people were very, very angry, but I knew the ones who were angry were the ones who were dishonest. After the deed was done—and I took a lot of flak for it—others came up and said, 'We didn't trust him.'"

The Busang drill cores were transported in wooden boxes to base camp and laid out on a concrete pad for logging, which was typically completed by a growing team of mostly Filipino geologists plus the odd Canadian. They would identify six-foot core sections that appeared to be mineralized, then crush and bag them for transport to the lab for assaying.

The process was later changed so that samples were floated downstream, where they were stored in a Bre-X warehouse. There, the sample bags, each composed of an inner plastic bag and outside fiberglass bag, were opened to confirm that they were properly described in the core logs and that no deterioration of the bags or samples had occurred from condensation or other causes. They typically accumulated at the Samarinda warehouse for weeks or even months while awaiting final inspection by de Guzman or Puspos before travelling by truck to the lab in Balikpapan. However, it was usually Puspos who signed the worksheets for the samples, as de Guzman was busy ferrying between the Bre-X office in Jakarta and other Bre-X exploration sites, and meeting with investors in Canada.

The Bre-X system of sampling the entire core was contrary to the standard mining protocol of splitting the core in half and retaining one half for later examination or re-assaying. Furthermore, although it is common to spot-check sample bags for integrity, opening both the inner and outer sample bag after they left the drill site was contrary to standard operating practices. Opening the outside bag would not have been a concern if the inside bag had remained closed.

Meanwhile, despite de Guzman's bustling schedule, he continued to accumulate more wives and even adopted new religions to do so. He married his third wife in 1995, a Bre-X employee named Susani who worked in the company's Manado office. To convince her, he converted to Islam and changed his name to Ismail Daud, a gesture that went beyond the requirements of Islamic protocol.

He married his fourth wife roughly a year later, a twenty-one-year-old named Lilis who worked at the Bre-X office in Samarinda. He wooed her with gifts and took her out for meals followed by karaoke duets. This time he adopted Protestantism as an overture to his bride. Their wedding was followed by a reception for three hundred guests, none of them de Guzman's friends or family as, according to Lilis's subsequent account, they were too difficult to contact.

In the event he hadn't created enough stress for himself at this point, health issues often left him debilitated. He had survived fourteen bouts of malaria, one of which landed him in the hospital for a month. According to Susani, he was frequently drenched in sweat and overcome with pain in his kidneys and liver. He had ballooned from 150 to 200 pounds a few years earlier, and in January 1997 he again checked himself into a hospital in Samarinda, this time complaining of chest pains. While he was hospitalized, a fire broke out at Busang, destroying the survey office where the drill logs were kept. Despite the fire having started around five a.m., Alo and Puspos blamed it on the air conditioner and photocopier overloading the electrical system. Before the site could be investigated, Alo showed up with a bulldozer and levelled everything still standing.

Shortly after being discharged from the hospital, de Guzman disappeared for a few days without notifying colleagues. Later, according to Diane Francis's book *Bre-X: The Inside Story*, he confided in a few people that he had been abducted in front of the apartment of a "girlfriend" (possibly his second wife, Genie) on the outskirts of Jakarta, blindfolded and held captive for several days. The girlfriend's brother was alleged to be a high-ranking official in the Indonesian government, and one of de Guzman's confidants theorized that he was being leaned on by the Indonesia military for protection money. He never reported the abduction to police or his company because he "understood the message being given to him," and he couldn't leave Bre-X.

Shortly thereafter, according to Jennifer Wells's account in her book *Fever: The Dark Mystery of the Bre-X Gold Rush*, de Guzman entertained his mother, two sisters and his first wife, Teresa, at the Shangri-La Hotel in Jakarta. He gave them a tour of the Bre-X offices, took them out for dinner and drove them through the countryside. Wells writes that the excursion also included a visit to a place where de Guzman had previously skydived, something he had taken up about ten years earlier "to relax." When asked why he had given it up, he replied: "Because I don't want to die with my body scattered all over the place." (The magnitude of the irony in that statement in light of subsequent events led me to confirm it with Wells.) Later he alluded to some sort of sabotage effort directed at Bre-X and said he had to watch his back. He explained that Bre-X had hired someone to investigate further, and on March 6 he phoned his mother to express his continuing concern: "Pray for me, Mama. They want to kill me."

On March 7, 1997, when de Guzman flew to Toronto for the four-day PDAC conference, he was joined by Puspos and Alo and two other Filipino geologists from the Bre-X team. After conference sessions, the group escaped the cold weather at a strip club called For Your Eyes Only. De Guzman and Puspos got to know two dancers, Maria and Michelle, roommates from Romania, and bought them Cristal champagne and took them shopping.

At this point de Guzman's first wife, Teresa, was in Quezon City (part of Metro Manila), caring for their six children; his second wife, Genie, was in the Jakarta outskirts, looking after their two children; his third wife, Susani, was in Manado with their son; and his fourth wife, Lilis, was in Samarinda. But apparently it wasn't enough that he had four wives and nine children spread over two countries, because he showed up at Maria's home with flowers and a ring to propose. She declined, but he left his phone number and address in the Philippines with her in case she changed her mind.

During the conference, de Guzman called an Australian friend who had helped him get an Australian residency stamp: the increasingly paranoid geologist was planning to move his first family there after they were threatened earlier that winter. De Guzman had made plans to visit Australia in a couple of weeks, and told his friend he was looking forward to it.

On March 12, the PDAC festivities were interrupted by the call from Freeport CEO Jim Bob Moffett about the problems they were encountering with the Busang drilling results. The Bre-X geologists had to abandon their plans to sightsee at Niagara Falls with the Romanian dancers, and instead flew back to Indonesia via Hong Kong. De Guzman, who was in first class, found himself sitting next to another PDAC conference attendee who happened to be friends with a Freeport executive. According to Brian Hutchinson's account in *Fools' Gold*, the passenger recalled that Alo and another man came forward from business class to discuss money with de Guzman, and it escalated into an argument. Apparently he had pocketed about $5 million and Alo, like the other Bre-X geologists attending the conference, had only received around $1 million.

In Hong Kong, de Guzman parted ways with the other Bre-X geologists and flew to Singapore to review results of his recent medical tests. He spent two days there with his second wife, Genie. Most of the test results were in the normal range—cholesterol a little elevated, so he was told to cut back on dairy and beef—but his hepatitis B assays were reason for some concern. If the results remained positive for over six months, he would be considered a hepatitis B carrier, meaning his blood would likely be infectious, putting him at greater risk of chronic liver disease. However, the doctor assured him, many people live normal lives as hepatitis B carriers.

From Singapore, de Guzman flew to Jakarta and then to Balikpapan, where he planned to catch a helicopter the next day to the Busang site. Rudy Vega, a Bre-X metallurgist with whom he wanted to discuss the discrepancies in the drilling results, met him in Balikpapan, and the two checked into a hotel together after picking up some cough syrup, as de Guzman was battling a cold. From the hotel, de Guzman sent his secretary in Jakarta a fax about various business matters, and also disclosed that he had passed his medical tests but had been advised to consult with a specialist regarding his liver. He told her he'd be in Jakarta on the 23rd or 24th.

According to Vega, the two of them then ventured out for dinner, followed by a visit to a karaoke bar, where de Guzman sang a few songs, including one of his favourites, "My Way." In the morning, de Guzman phoned an administrative assistant at the Bre-X offices in Manado and instructed her to have twenty million rupiahs (around US$10,000 at the time) in cash ready for Susani to pick up. Then he phoned Lilis to inform her that he was travelling to Busang and asked if she could book a table for them to go out for dinner in Samarinda to celebrate their first wedding anniversary upon his return. Finally, he phoned Genie and asked if she could pick him up at the airport in Jakarta on March 21.

De Guzman and Vega then took a taxi to the airport, where the helicopter was waiting. According to Vega, de Guzman muttered a few times: "Shit, I shouldn't have done this. This was the second time." When Vega inquired, de Guzman said he had fallen asleep in the bathtub after drinking the cough medicine. Vega later told investigators that "it was my impression Michael had tried to commit suicide that night." They arrived over an hour late for their flight, which was atypical for the normally punctual geologist. He was wearing shorts, a t-shirt and a jean jacket.

The aircraft they boarded, a French-designed Alouette III utility helicopter outfitted with six passenger seats, belonged to Indonesian Air Transport, a subsidiary of a holding company owned by Suharto's son Bambang. The pilot was a lieutenant-colonel in the Indonesian Army named Edy Tursono (some sources spell it "Edi"), who according to some reports was still actively serving in the army while moonlighting with the company; he was accompanied by a co-pilot.

They stopped at Samarinda to refuel. Vega and de Guzman headed into the airport lounge, where they were met by two Bre-X employees, one of them reportedly Alo. The manifest showed both passengers would be continuing to Busang, but only de Guzman returned to the helicopter, explaining that Vega would be staying behind. As the now-solo passenger boarded the helicopter, he was now wearing jeans.

The helicopter took off and Tursono climbed to a cruising altitude of eight hundred feet. Twenty minutes into the flight there was a pop, followed by a bang and a rush of air from the back as the helicopter jolted upwards. The co-pilot looked back and saw that the rear left door was open and de Guzman was gone.

"It was damn considerate of him to jump from the left side," the helicopter company's general manager later remarked. "Had he gone from the right, he would have struck the rotors and brought the chopper down."

The pilots recorded the location and flew back and forth over the jungle canopy in search of the spot where he may have landed, but it was a futile effort and they returned to Samarinda after twenty-five minutes. The pair was questioned by police for seven hours, but the police chief said he was not allowed to discuss the case publicly because "it is very sensitive. It is close to the son of our leader." Tursono's testimony was later revised by the police, according to Jakarta journalist Manuela Saragosa, to state that he saw de Guzman jump after writing notes. Also suspicious was an account unearthed by *Wall Street Journal* reporters Peter Waldman and Jay Solomon: according to Bre-X employees who wished to remain anonymous, an unknown individual joined de Guzman on the flight after Vega departed.

Left behind in de Guzman's baggage, which included three cases of Bintang beer, were various notes. One of them included the following messages:

Authorization Letter
Full Authority given to Mr Bernhard Leode [Bre-X's Jakarta-based financial controller] *to represent, act on my behalf and, for my behalf in case of disability or my death. Voluntarily issued 18 March 1997.*

Sweetheart, Thess 18/3/97
Mahal [dearest loved one], *I must leave you now. I am very sorry. My sickness is killing me. I tried my best for you and our children – please forgive me for my misgivings*

Mahal, you MUST BE STRONG and CONTINUE. I will die without regrets – LORD GOD HAVE BLESS US MORE THAN EVER. I LOVE YOU, I LOVE OUR CHILDREN. WATCH YOUR HEALTH.

Love Forever Mike.

To: My Children 18/3/97
I love all of you. Mama loves all of you. We love all of you. Please love your Mama. Respect her, be loyal to her, protect her at all time. Protect each of you. I will leave all of you due to my sickness. My request, Pls. protect your Mama – All of you, all the time. Years, years.

The granting of power of attorney to Bernhard Leode, a power that wouldn't survive de Guzman's death, included a peculiar attempt at forging Leode's signature as a countersigner. It also specified "in case of disability or my death," which was curious wording for someone about to jump from a helicopter. The message to his wife Teresa was noteworthy, as he referred to her as "Thess" instead of the usual "Tess." He also referred to the sickness "killing him," presumably hepatitis B, despite the relatively benign diagnosis.

There were also similar messages to de Guzman's sons, Birl and Mike Jr., ordering them to look after their mother, and instructions to Teresa to sell the boats and the apartment they owned if she needed money. Another note was written with very large block lettering so that it took up six pages. It contained the following messages:

MY FINAL REQUEST TO RUDY – RM 914
PLS BRING MY BLACK BAG W/ALL MY VERY IMPORTANT
NOTES
MUST HAND CARRY TO OFFICE AND BOGOR KEY HERE.
THANKS
Mike

TO: MR. JOHN FELDERHOF + ALL MY FRIENDS
SORRY I HAVE TO LEAVE I CANNOT THINK OF MYSELF AS
A CARRIER OF HEPATITIS "B" I CANNOT JEOPARDISE YOUR
LIFES, SAME W/ MY LOVED ONES.

GOD BLESS YOU ALL No more stomach pains!! No more
back pains!!

TO BERNARD FOR MY WIFE TERESA. MY REQUEST DO NOT BURY ME BURN – CREMATE ME IN MANILA

Bernhard Leode
*Pls accompany my body (death) to Manila Documents for my wife Teresa - Pls hand carry including my passport
*In Jkt - Do not bring my body to Bogor.
Stay at Funeral Parlor while waiting for Travel to Manila.

*Settle accounts
Personal
Thank you very much
My dear friend.

These messages also raised questions. For one thing, there was no reason for him to fear spreading hepatitis B, as he would only need to wear a condom and avoid donating blood, and his condition would most likely have been cured with time. There was also the peculiarity of putting "death" in brackets after the reference to the body, as if clarification was needed.

It took four days for rescue teams and Bre-X employees to beat through the dense bush to find de Guzman's badly disfigured and decomposed body. Insects, maggots and wild boars had all picked away at it. Missing were part of the scalp, an eye, most teeth, the genitals, chest bones and internal organs. Alo reportedly helped with the search and provided the identification based on a lump on the left shoulder. De Guzman's fourth wife, Lilis, later reviewed photographs of the body and confirmed the identification on the same basis. Dental records were not used, fingerprint evidence was inconclusive and DNA tests were never completed.

Indonesian authorities concluded that de Guzman died by "dropping himself from the helicopter." The RCMP, which also investigated the death, agreed. Filipino authorities announced that the matter was classified. Other observers, however, described the Indonesian investigation as shoddy and said it led to more questions than answers.

After de Guzman's death, rumours began to circulate that Freeport had not found the Busang gold, yet the stock price remained at lofty levels. Bre-X maintained de Guzman had committed suicide for personal reasons, faulting his "terminal" hepatitis B diagnosis as the ultimate trigger, and they continued to express confidence in the company's published resource estimates.

However, on March 19 the Bre-X board directed the company to retain Strathcona Mineral Services to complete an independent audit of the Busang drilling results. Graham Farquharson, a well-respected veteran geologist, spent a couple of days in Jakarta reviewing documents, including the Freeport results. Even before drilling any holes, he concluded that material information was being withheld from the market. He phoned his wife, who had been his secretary for eighteen years: "Get out your pad and take down the most significant letter you've ever taken down in your career or my career. Fax it to me for double-checking, then we'll get it downtown [Toronto] by nine a.m."

Farquharson's statement read: "Based on the work done by Freeport and our own review and observations to date, there appears to be a strong possibility that the potential gold resources on the Busang property have been overstated because of invalid samples and assaying thereof."

The trading of shares was halted for almost two days as Walsh lobbied the stock exchange to suspend trading indefinitely while due diligence was completed. His request was denied. When the statement was released, over $3 billion of the company's market value, roughly 80 per cent, quickly evaporated. Still, Walsh refused to concede: "I am 120 per cent confident that the gold is there and that there has been a colossal screw-up."

About a month and the drilling of six test holes later, Strathcona's final report was made available, and it concluded that an economic gold deposit in Busang's southeast zone was unlikely and that "the magnitude of the tampering with core samples that we believe has occurred and the resulting falsification of assay values at Busang is of a scale and over a period of time and with a precision that, to our knowledge, is without precedent in the history of mining anywhere in the world."

When trading resumed, the stock opened at eighty cents, and the exchange had to shut down for an hour as 58 million shares traded, roughly 50 per cent more than the exchange's previous single day record. A few days later the stock was delisted from exchanges, and the company was forced into bankruptcy later that year.

———————————————

It was while Bre-X was unravelling that Walsh allegedly hired Bjornstrom. They met in Walsh's office in Bre-X's headquarters, a four-storey red brick building across the river from downtown Calgary with the company name displayed on the exterior in large gold letters. Bjornstrom was given files to review, and Walsh arranged for him to travel to Indonesia.

Bjornstrom was only one of several investigators Bre-X deployed to Indonesia and the Philippines to interview workers, geologists, pilots, airport employees, widows, gold panners and others. Testifying at his trial, Bjornstrom said he was sent on a three-day trip by Walsh roughly a week and a half after de Guzman was reported dead, travelling through Vancouver and Manila to Jakarta, where he was met by a Bre-X employee. He interviewed several people associated with de Guzman and visited the Busang site before travelling back to Manila and then home.

Bjornstrom claimed to have uncovered information suggesting de Guzman was pushed from the helicopter and was already dead at the time, or at least nearly dead. He suggested that one or more people working for Indonesian business and political interests were behind the murder. The only information he provided as evidence was that a military pilot had been assigned to fly de Guzman, since the regular pilot was mysteriously unavailable. Bjornstrom said he reported back to Walsh that he believed de Guzman was murdered.

After returning from Indonesia, Bjornstrom said he was in his Calgary office when he was confronted by individuals connected to Bre-X. "Some men came into my office near the end of the day on a Friday," he said. "Based on the line of questioning, I sensed it was not going to end well. Two of them grabbed me and started working me over and the third one went and removed the hard drives from my computers." They also took all the files, diskettes and photographs he had collected relating to Bre-X. They threatened him and his family with further harm before leaving him "bruised and sore from head to toe."

CHAPTER 8

AFTER THE GOLD RUSH

> ❝ I know the secrets behind the Bre-X collapse and there is a reward
> from overseas to see my extinction."
>
> Note left by **John Bjornstrom** in a visitors' diary in a cabin near
> Shuswap Lake, dated August 27, 2000

Bre-X shortened more than one life. Roughly a year after
the company unravelled, David Walsh succumbed to a brain
aneurysm at his oceanfront retreat in the Bahamas, his death
presumably hastened by the stress of the scandal. Investor
Lawrence Beadle, a recently retired criminal lawyer living in
the Lower Mainland, shot himself after losing $3 million and,
according to his wife, being overcome with depression. And
a guilt-ridden stockbroker named Pierre Turgeon jumped
from his seventh-floor apartment after encouraging clients to
invest in Bre-X, including a close friend who lost most of his
life savings.

Nobody ever went to jail for direct involvement in the scam, and after seventeen years of litigation associated with several class action lawsuits, no funds were ever returned to hoodwinked investors. An RCMP investigation was abandoned in 1999, as most of the witnesses were spread across four countries outside of Canada and couldn't be compelled to testify. "I'm quite comfortable that I know how it happened," said Peter Macaulay, the RCMP investigator who oversaw the case. "It's just we can never prove it. And will we ever be able to? Not unless one of the insiders decided to confess the whole thing, and I can't see why they would."

The consensus of those who knew Walsh was that, despite having promoted the Busang claims assiduously, he had paid little attention to the details of the drilling operation, rarely visited the site and had no knowledge of the salting operation. Court filings showed his estate was essentially bankrupt and faced a $33 million charge from the Canada Revenue Agency for outstanding taxes. His widow, Jeannette, is reported to be living a quiet life in an apartment on an island near Nassau, and her sons both work in the film industry overseas.

The Ontario Securities Commission (OSC) charged John Felderhof with trading on inside information when he and his wife sold $84 million in Bre-X shares, and with authorizing misleading press releases. He faced up to sixteen years in jail and $8 million in fines on top of potentially three times the profits he garnered from insider trading. The trial commenced in 2000 and included 157 days of testimony from various officials, consultants, experts, geologists, Bre-X officers and directors, plus Peter Munk, chairman of Barrick. There were over 190 binders of documents and fifteen thousand pages of transcripts. "If I read all day five days a week," the judge commented, "it would still take me four or five months just to get through the transcript."

Much of the case against Felderhof relied upon twenty red flags identified in a report by Strathcona Mineral Services, indications of tampering that should have alerted him to wrongdoing. According to Strathcona, the salting process was very simple, and most of the roughly twenty-five-thousand-plus samples that were tampered with would have been salted at the Samarinda warehouse. Someone there had opened the bags and supplemented the samples with precisely measured amounts of gold before sending them off for final testing. More than one player had to be involved, as coordination was required between the completion of the drill logs at the Busang site and salting of the samples at Samarinda. The Strathcona report suggested that Dayak gold panners were the source of the salting gold, allegedly purchased from a *warung*, or small shop, close to Busang and estimated to have cost about US$25,000 in total.

The defence called Munk, who asserted he was overcome with "disbelief and horror" when he learned of the Busang results. "It never occurred to me once," he said, "that a fraud of this magnitude could be possibly happening in a country as developed in the mining industry as Canada." Several experts testified that the red flags identified by Strathcona were not red flags at all. Geologist Phillip Hellman disagreed that the salting gold had been purchased from a *warung*, citing geochemical fingerprinting tests he had completed on gold panned from nearby streams. He testified that "the very first drill logs I looked at had visible gold there." The defence cited a 1996 independent review by one of North America's best known and respected mineral auditing groups, which found that the Busang work was "being done to a high standard."

The decision of the court, which was finally rendered in 2007, seven years after the trial commenced, found Felderhof not guilty of any charges. The judge concluded that Strathcona's findings had the benefit of hindsight and that Felderhof had demonstrated a level of diligence to the industry standard. *The Northern Miner* questioned the decision and asserted that Strathcona had been unfairly savaged by the bulldog defence lawyer, Joseph Groia, who was able to sow seeds of doubt with his tangential arguments. Indeed, in 2012 a law society discipline panel convicted Groia of professional misconduct for the incivility he had displayed during the trial. He appealed the decision all the way to the Supreme Court and was vindicated in 2018, despite the court admonishing him for regularly deploying "rhetorical excess and sarcasm," "petulant invective" and "guerilla theatre."

John Felderhof's second wife, Ingrid, told *The Globe and Mail* that her husband grew bitter and resentful throughout the lawsuits and criminal trial and became consumed with firing off angry faxes, his preferred mode of communication. "A lot of our relationship was based on faxes," she said, and she kept two drawers in her home for them. "One was for good faxes, one for bad." Their marriage eventually succumbed to the toll of the Bre-X aftermath and they divorced. She kept the Cayman Island properties—the Lamborghini and other properties were sold to pay his legal costs— and maintained she knew nothing about the $84 million he was supposed to have pocketed from selling shares. She has her own theory regarding de Guzman's death: he was murdered by the helicopter pilots, who were working for the Indonesian intelligence agency. In her opinion, de Guzman was too happy to choose suicide.

John Felderhof died of natural causes in October 2019, at the age of 79. He had been living in the Philippines in a two-bedroom whitewashed cement home with his third wife, Maria, her four children and one grandchild. "I've gone from having millions to this," he confessed to *The Northern Miner*, "but Maria and I could be happy together living on nothing." They operated a convenience store out of the main level of their house and a restaurant out of the kitchen, supplementing that income by selling rice and renting out the roof.

He was apprehensive to learn that a movie, *Gold*, was to be made about Bre-X, as he was concerned about its accuracy. Eventually he agreed to serve as a technical adviser, but how much input he had is questionable: the movie strays considerably from actual events, which in this case were arguably more intriguing than the Hollywood version. He'd had plenty of time to reflect on what happened at Busang and claimed it took fifteen of those years to figure out how the salting was carried out and by whom. Other than specifying that he didn't believe de Guzman was involved, he refused to reveal any names: "I know what it's like to be accused. It's easy to accuse and destroy a person's life, but I have no proof, so I won't accuse them. I'm not going to point fingers at anybody."

Graham Farquharson is still at the helm of Strathcona Mineral Services and a member of the Canadian Mining Hall of Fame. When I asked him if anything has emerged to change his conclusions, he said nothing had changed, including his disbelief that it took three and a half years for the truth to emerge. After delivering its first report, his firm had been asked to investigate who had carried out the salting program and concluded that "De Guzman and his staff were very much involved in coordinating the whole program." He also thinks Felderhof, given his extensive experience, must have known what was occurring. In his opinion the only mystery that remains is what happened to de Guzman.

The man who completed the autopsy of the body alleged to be that of de Guzman, Dr. Daniel Umar, now says he is uncertain if it was the geologist's body that was found in the jungle. At the time he accepted it as de Guzman's body because that is what the police told him. "The autopsy was done not to find out whose body it was," he told *Calgary Herald* journalist Suzanne Wilton, "but to justify the way he died." If he carried out the autopsy today, he would collect DNA.

Genie, the second of de Guzman's wives, believes he is still alive. In a 2005 interview with journalist John McBeth—which she gave despite a warning from military police not to give any interviews after de Guzman's death—she disclosed that she had received funds from her supposedly dead husband. He had, she said, phoned her house a month after his apparent demise and relayed through her maid that he had deposited funds in her account, where she later discovered US$200,000. On the anniversary of his birthday, February 14, 2005, she received a fax in his handwriting notifying her of another US$25,000 in her account sent from a Brazilian Citibank branch.

Brian King is a private investigator who was hired by a film production company in 2007 to look into Genie's story and other evidence that de Guzman is enjoying life in Brazil or some other hideaway. The company's intent was to make a documentary for CBC, but the public broadcaster pulled the funding before it was completed. When I reached King, he was happy to share some of his findings. After explaining that his past work had included surveillance for Barrick in their pursuit of the Busang gold, he told me he had travelled to Indonesia to meet with Genie and get copies of the bank deposit records, but the project's funding was cut before he could confirm they were accurate. She told him de Guzman was carrying US$300,000 in cash when he left her just before the helicopter flight, and the money was never found. King also interviewed Dr. Umar, who told him the body did not have the telltale shoulder lump. As well, King learned that a body was stolen from a nearby morgue around the same time.

Genie's claims support the theory that de Guzman faked his death out of compassion for his wives. One of his friends, a schoolmate from the Philippines who lived in Samarinda, acknowledged that whereas his friend was indeed incorrigible, in his opinion he was also a man of principle. Rather than just having flings with the women in his life, he married them and supported them financially. Other geologists operating in remote areas of that region were known to do the same thing, faking their deaths upon parting and leaving a financial gift as a form of life insurance. This achieved multiple objectives: the wife's dignity was left intact, she was financially set and as a widow she was free to remarry.

Alfred Lenarciak, a Polish-born Canadian, was chairman of the mining company Minorca Resources, which had a stake in Bre-X. He wrote a book about the saga in which he describes a chance encounter in 2012 at a church in Rome with a familiar-looking man who introduced himself as Akiro Guzzo. They agreed to meet up for lunch a week later, and in the meantime the author began to wonder if the man was really de Guzman, whom he had last seen singing "My Way" in a hotel bar in Hong Kong. Over lunch, Guzzo asked Lenarciak if he knew who he was, and when Lenarciak responded affirmatively, it was agreed they would talk about any previous events in the third person.

Guzzo proceeded to tell de Guzman's story, beginning with salting the first sample— using gold he had purchased to make a cross for his youngest daughter's first communion—in order to buy some time for the project and himself. The scam had spiralled from there, as had his elaborate plan to extricate himself—it involved Opus Dei, the secretive Catholic organization, and an illegitimate son he had fathered with a girl in Opus Youth, who had fled the country in shame. It was ultimately an associate from Opus Dei who helped him slip into Italy on his way back from the PDAC conference in Toronto and, with the help of a little plastic surgery, take on his new identity as Akiro Guzzo, the son of a Filipina and a Japanese pilot shot down in the Philippines in World War II.

Then came the matter of faking his death. De Guzman phoned the Bre-X office in Jakarta from Italy, telling them he had landed in Singapore. He was informed that it wasn't just Freeport looking for him; Suharto's secret police, known as BIN, were also hunting for him. De Guzman phoned Puspos's brother Manny, who also worked for Bre-X, and asked Manny to meet him in Singapore and accompany him to Jakarta. Upon arriving in Singapore, however, Manny was informed that de Guzman was in the hospital, and he was asked instead to deliver a sealed envelope to the Bre-X office in Jakarta. That envelope contained the suicide notes. Manny was picked up at the Jakarta airport by BIN officers who were expecting de Guzman.

Freeport had informed Bob Hasan that there was no meaningful quantity of gold at Busang. Hasan had relayed the news to Suharto, who did not respond well. Hasan understood that those responsible would have to be punished. He didn't know *whom* to punish though, and he landed on the theory that de Guzman was working for a Filipino organized crime group known as the Kuratong Mafia. Eager to send a message to the Kuratong and, devoid of compelling options, Hasan settled on staging de Guzman's suicide with the help of the geologist's own suicide notes.

So at the Balikpapan hangar a cadaver was loaded onto the Alouette helicopter and heaved into the jungle. Vega and the flight crew were forced to go along with a concocted story of their final hours with de Guzman. However, the corpse that took the place of de Guzman's body was Indonesian, which created an issue as it was circumcised—Indonesian males, unlike Catholic Filipinos, are typically circumcised—so the errant appendage was removed before the corpse was tossed from the helicopter.

It is unclear what is fiction and what is non-fiction in Lenarciak's story, and he never responded to my attempts to contact him. He followed up his initial book with another version, *Gold of Bre-X*, published five years later, which corrected many of the grammar and spelling errors found in his first version. That may have been the principal reason for reissuing it, but the new version also added a curious epilogue about running into Akiro Guzzo again, this time singing "My Way" in an Istanbul hotel bar. Guzzo commended the author on his first book but suggested some editing and the addition of some new elements. Lenarciak told him that "my Bre-X story will stand as written. If you want something new, then it is up to you to write it." The conversation ended with Guzzo saying he would be in touch.

De Guzman's youngest brother, Simplicio, the de facto family spokesperson, also questioned whether his brother committed suicide. He pointed to letters found in his brother's bag that detailed things he expected to do over the following days and pointed out infelicities in the suicide notes, including the lack of any mention of his mother, the most important woman in his brother's world. Other questions plagued Simplicio: Why did his brother board the helicopter alone? Why did he change clothes before supposedly killing himself? Why was he making arrangements to move to Australia with his family?

Some family members hired Dr. Jerome Bailen, a forensic anthropologist and associate professor of anthropology at the University of the Philippines, to lead an investigation team that included another anthropologist and a medical doctor. Their twenty-three-page report hypothesizes that de Guzman was forced to disclose information about Busang, compelled to write his suicide notes and then executed. His body was then tossed from the helicopter to fabricate a suicide, while also serving to silence others with knowledge of the salting scam. Part of the basis for this theory was the corpse's missing internal organs, which the team believed were removed to inhibit determination of the cause of death. They also noted the lack of blood pooling around fractures, as pooling would have been expected had the tissue been alive at the time the bones broke. Horizontal imprints along the back and neck supported their assertion that he was strangled with a ligature, "garrote style," while restrained in a chair. The report goes on to speculate that the perpetrators were probably the same individuals from the Indonesian military who had allegedly kidnapped de Guzman the previous year to obtain information about Bre-X.

CHAPTER 9

THE HIT LIST

The issue of there being an assassination contract against [Bjornstrom] from Bre-X appears to have been confirmed by news sources. So, while it initially appears to be quite bizarre, it seems to be supported by the facts."

Don Campbell, Bjornstrom's lawyer, speaking to news media on January 12, 2004

Seemingly every greying man I come across has a Bre-X story to share: "Oh, you know Terry who lived down the street, he lost $300k" or "Have you heard of the small town in northern Alberta where most people bought in after the local credit union loans officer recommended it and then lost their entire savings?" Occasionally, it's a boast from the other side of the ledger about getting out in time: "Bre-X paid for my [renovation / second home / etc.]." Other stories were more conspiratorial in nature, and I wasn't sure what to make of them. The story that most bewildered me though, was Rob Nicholson's account of how he met Bjornstrom.

I had joined the affable retired private investigator and purveyor of Bushman documents in Kelowna for lunch at

Denny's, and among the many things he left me to ponder was his story of Pitt Lake's Lost Gold Mine—and the possibility of its mysterious entanglement with Bre-X. Nicholson, who comes from a long lineage of prospectors, began prospecting in his early teens. He first heard of the Lost Gold Mine in the late 1980s, when he was drilling and blasting for a logging operation near Pitt Lake. The twenty-five-kilometre-long tidal lake, the same one where Bjornstrom had set up camp as a twelve-year-old, drains into the lower Fraser River east of New Westminster.

Nicholson's interest in the Lost Gold Mine culminated in his 2002 book, *Lost Creek Mine: Historical Analysis of the Legendary Gold Deposit of Pitt Lake*, which begins with the story of a Katzie First Nations man named Slumach who would disappear into the rugged wilderness beyond Pitt Lake and reappear weeks or months later with a small fortune in gold, which he would disburse in various establishments in New Westminster. He was hanged in 1891 after being convicted of murdering a man named Louis Bee on the shores of Pitt River. (Nicholson reviewed the trial transcript and other documents and lays out a plausible self-defence argument for Slumach that was not presented during the trial.) Before being sent to the gallows, he never revealed the location of what has come to be known as Slumach's gold.

The next character in the story, also known by a single name, Jackson, was a veteran prospector who set out to find the source of Slumach's gold and returned with a rucksack filled with over $8,000 worth of nuggets that he deposited in a San Francisco bank. Shortly thereafter he succumbed to a fatal illness, but before his death he wrote a letter that vaguely described the location as a difficult two- or three-day hike from Pitt Lake. Many individuals have since tried to find that location.

Stuart Brown was one of them. A veteran of World War II, he survived seventeen bombing missions over Germany as a navigator and twenty-one months in a German prisoner of war camp. After the war he was working on a thesis on the sawfly for a master's degree that led him to the Pitt Lake area. A friend suggested they do some prospecting while on a break, and he was drawn into the legend of the Lost Gold Mine, but it wasn't until 1973 that he found time to work on it more earnestly.

By that time Brown was supervising an Environment Canada survey section that involved close inspection of aerial photos—a skill he had honed navigating bombers—and he found a site that was nearly an exact match for the location described by Jackson. After visiting it in person, he claimed to have waded in gold nuggets up to his ankles. It was within Garibaldi Provincial Park, however, where mining was not allowed. He proposed that the provincial government extract the gold and use it to pay down government debt, but he was rebuffed.

Brown was not seeking personal gain. He wanted to see the gold used for the greatest public benefit, not siphoned away one $100,000 backpack load at a time, or even more rapaciously and at worse environmental cost. Although he didn't have much expertise to back up his estimate of the find's total value—somewhere between $1 billion and $20 billion—a man who authors such papers as *Selection for Forage and Avoidance of Risk by Woodland Caribou at Course and Local Scales* and *Estimating Moose Occurrence and Abundance from Remotely Derived Environmental Indicators* would seem to be a generally trustworthy sort.

Brown's correspondence with the provincial government over the years is amusing to read. They can't seem to fathom that anything notable could be discovered by a man who is not looking for personal gain and asks only that his expenses be reimbursed if the gold is found and that it be extracted in a minimally intrusive way. The correspondence culminates in a 1978 letter from Premier W.A.C. Bennett, who acknowledges the legend of the Lost Gold Mine, recognizes that the discovery has put Brown in a difficult position and then tells him, in effect, to bugger off.

Nicholson developed a relationship with Brown, and the two made a couple of attempts to visit the gold deposit but were thwarted by bad weather both times. They never actually set foot on a trail together before Brown developed Parkinson's disease and became disillusioned with his two-decade struggle to do the right thing. Nicholson tried once more to locate it on his own but was unsuccessful. He gave up on further attempts after developing some health issues.

After writing his book, Nicholson posted a couple of chapters on his website and subsequently received a mysterious call: "Get that material off the internet. It's interconnected with Bre-X, and if anyone knows about it, they're in serious trouble." Nicholson was perplexed, but what emerged from his fax machine forty-five minutes later truly frightened him: an obscure photo of him taken in 1977 while he was serving in a small independent military unit. The incredulity is still apparent in his voice when he recounts seeing the fax. Having followed the Bushman story in the local paper, he was aware of Bjornstrom's claim that threats related to Bre-X had driven him to the bush. He tracked down Bjornstrom's lawyer, Shawn Buckley, who was based in Kamloops.

While Buckley wasn't sure what to make of the mysterious call and fax, he did recognize that Nicholson might be able to assist with the investigative work necessary to prepare Bjornstrom's case for trial. Buckley had been doing work for Legal Aid at the time of Bjornstrom's arrest, though some negotiation had been required for him to represent Bjornstrom, as the standard arrangement for complex legal cases was to cover just sixty hours at seventy-two dollars per hour. Preparation for Bjornstrom's case could have easily required up to twice that amount of time, as well as more funding for the actual trial. Nicholson agreed to assist even though Legal Aid would not cover his costs.

Buckley later dropped the case because, according to Nicholson, he became concerned for his family's safety.

When I reached out to Buckley for any insights he could share, his first response was to ask me if I knew about "the letter." Nicholson had already told me about a letter from the Indonesian police referring to a hit list connected to Bre-X that had Bjornstrom's name on it. I asked if that was the letter he was referring to, and he responded affirmatively and said he would need some time to consider whether he was willing to help me. The next time I reached him, he said he was unable to assist. He would not specify why.

The only other reference I've encountered to anyone else finding their way onto a Bre-X hit list was in Alfred Lenarciak's account of his purported conversation with de Guzman living as Akiro Guzzo in Milan—so it should be treated accordingly. Guzzo believed that Suharto and his cronies anticipated massive proceeds from Bre-X and were both enraged and embarrassed when it was revealed to be a hoax. A hit list was put together, and it included Walsh who was, according to Guzzo, murdered in his Bahamas home.

There were indeed suspicious events surrounding Walsh's death. Three weeks earlier, according to the *Calgary Herald*, two men had barged into his bedroom, tied him up and threatened to kill him unless he turned over all his money. The beleaguered Walsh suggested they go downstairs and check out his desk: "Look at all of the statements of claim against me. You'll see I don't have any money." They left without incident and were later arrested. Then, while Walsh's funeral was taking place in Montreal, his house in the Bahamas was broken into after a man posing as a family member phoned the security company to cancel the guard. Shortly thereafter, a family friend arrived at the house and surprised an intruder, who quickly fled, leaving files strewn about but no valuables missing.

While the first of these incidents may have accelerated the underlying causes that led to Walsh's brain aneurysm, there is no basis to assume either was directly connected with his death. Rather, his lifestyle seemed to be the most likely culprit, as high blood pressure, smoking and excessive alcohol consumption can all be contributing factors.

Lenarciak, whose company became a part owner of the Busang project, wonders if he too was on a hit list. He claims that in the aftermath of the Strathcona report, while he was winding down his company's Indonesian operations, he was summoned to a meeting with Bob Hasan in Jakarta. He wasn't told the reason for the meeting, but he was headed to Jakarta anyway. As the vehicle he was riding in approached the Jakarta hotel, it was stopped by the police, who pointed a machine gun at him and asked for his name. Lenarciak gave a fake name and the police signalled the driver to continue. When he got to the hotel, he was told a room was reserved for him and he was not to leave it, as someone would join him there. Instead, he got off the elevator on a different floor, left the hotel on foot, grabbed a taxi for the airport and fled the country.

The Kijiji package I bought from Rob Nicholson includes a one-page statement from Bjornstrom regarding Bre-X. It begins by describing the Busang find and goes on to lay out a byzantine scheme by the Canadian government to use Bre-X as an alternative financing vehicle to invest in Indonesia while avoiding the credit constraints of continued lending to that country. Later in the signed statement, Bjornstrom states there were two other individuals on de Guzman's final helicopter ride, and one of them was Suharto's son Tommy.

At Bjornstrom's trial, the lawyer who ultimately represented him, Don Campbell, attempted to provide evidence of a connection between his client and Tommy in the form of a news report that suggested Tommy had put out an assassination contract on Bjornstrom. The report was originally given to Bjornstrom's first lawyer, Shawn Buckley, by the prosecutor. Upon receiving it, Buckley had retained a CNN Indonesian correspondent named David Ireland to validate its legitimacy. Ireland reported back that in his opinion it came from a legitimate source. However, the judge at Bjornstrom's trial deemed the report inadmissible because he was concerned about its reliability, which ironically stemmed from questions raised by the prosecutor who first unearthed the report.

While Tommy had not been publicly associated with the wrangling for control of Bre-X, he was involved behind closed doors, according to another private investigator. When Barrick was angling for control of Busang, an investigator hired by Bre-X advised that Barrick was holding secret negotiations with Suharto family members. "The President's son, Tommy, is taking an interest," relayed the investigator, according to evidence presented at Felderhof's trial. "Tommy has instructed Bob Nasution, a senior member at the attorney general's office, to create political problems for [Bre-X] in Indonesia . . . This is a very delicate situation."

Of all the Suharto children, Tommy was seemingly most at ease with the family's approach to pillaging the country. He was also the most likely to react violently when things didn't go his way. For example, Tommy was caught making a minor side deal in which he helped a car-racing companion secure land for a hypermarket in Jarkarta by orchestrating the swap of remote, polluted swampland for prime real estate owned by an ostensibly state-controlled entity. This was insignificant relative to his other swindles, but it was viewed as an easier case to prosecute.

Attempts at putting Tommy on trial were subsequently thwarted by changes in witnesses' testimony and, later, explosions in public places that police were instructed not to investigate. Further attempts at prosecuting him simmered until several years later. After Suharto resigned in 1998, the public became increasingly aware of how much of the nation's wealth his family had siphoned away, and he was put on trial a couple of years later. Tommy was questioned as a witness, and an hour after his testimony a bomb exploded nearby. A few months later, with Suharto's trial set to resume, a bomb exploded in the basement parkade of the Jakarta Stock Exchange, killing fifteen people. Tommy was suspected of being involved but was not questioned (the police chief was later fired for refusing to do so), so instead he was arrested for his involvement in the land scam.

Tommy was sentenced to eighteen months in prison by the Supreme Court, but instead of serving the sentence he went into hiding; then, after trying unsuccessfully to bribe Indonesia's new president and the lead judge to overturn his sentence, he had the judge killed while he was on his way to work. Two hit men were paid US$11,000 and used a gun Tommy loaned them to shoot the judge from a motorcycle while he was stuck in traffic. The Supreme Court responded to the assassination by overturning Tommy's corruption conviction, a perplexing move suspected to be a ploy to entice him from hiding. Tommy did eventually emerge from hiding and was sentenced to fifteen years in jail for orchestrating the judge's murder, but he was only incarcerated for four years, some of that in a cell next to "Uncle Bob" Hassan, who was serving a sentence for unrelated corruption charges.

It's unclear what Tommy's motive would have been for having de Guzman murdered—if he was indeed murdered— and what led Bjornstrom to implicate him. When I spoke with Campbell, he could no longer recall any specifics of what he referred to as a letter from the Indonesian police describing a hit list with Bjornstrom's name on it. He could only say that he was convinced Bjornstrom had been working for Bre-X in some capacity: "What he said was sensible, and he seemed to be very knowledgeable. He possessed information that I wouldn't have expected him to have unless he was involved in the way he suggested." Bjornstrom's family members say he didn't tell them much about the work he did for Bre-X, preferring to shield them from it. They were only aware that he had been hired by David Walsh to investigate concerns regarding the integrity of the Bre-X operation and de Guzman's death, and that he had travelled to Indonesia at least once.

After Bjornstrom was confronted in his office, the threats allegedly continued, with insinuations that he and his family were "finished" if he said anything about Bre-X. In a later interview with the RCMP, he stated that he went to the police in Calgary, but they didn't take him seriously, one officer effectively asking what planet he was from while the other stared at the ceiling. "I would have had a better conversation talking to a wall," he said. Now overwhelmed by fear for himself and those associated with him, Bjornstrom decided to flee.

He had been living in a small rental house near a lot where he could park his truck. Next to that lot was a twenty-four-hour-a-day fast food joint called Donairs, where street kids—mostly teenagers but some as young as eleven—often hung out. He gradually got to know some of them, empathizing with their situations because he had been a runaway himself. "Some of them started coming over, a place to wash their clothes, get cleaned up, shower, bath, a clean bed to sleep in, a hot meal," he told the courtroom during his trial, "and then they'd carry on." In return they kept an eye on his truck.

One of the street kids was a girl who went by the name Alexis, and one day some of the kids showed up at his door to tell him that she had gone downtown and was planning to jump from a building. Bjornstrom was able to find her and convince her not to, and the next day she joined him on a trucking delivery and opened up to him. Gradually the other kids told him of their problems too, which often entailed physical and sexual abuse by people they trusted, leading them into alcohol, drugs and prostitution. Most of the time he just listened: "They're alone. They're out in the world and it's harsh, but they're alone." Several of the kids told him of being recruited to model for "movies"—child pornography—being made in the Shuswap area. They also spoke of a specific cabin there but were unable to provide details.

So when the threats related to Bre-X eventually overwhelmed him, Bjornstrom decided to flee to the Shuswap without much in the way of a plan or supplies, compelled to investigate the stories he had heard. Given his ill-preparedness, he opted to steal supplies by breaking into lakeside cabins, some of which he also stayed in. He established his camp in a grove of trees high on a hillside near the far end of Anstey Arm above Four Mile Creek. His shelter was a green tent covered with plastic sheeting, and he stocked it with a generator and power tools.

Given the near impassibility of the surrounding terrain, it was particularly perplexing that one of the items he stole was an all-terrain vehicle. How he managed to transport it up the lake is a mystery, though perhaps he towed it behind a canoe: the tires on an ATV are typically buoyant enough to keep it afloat, albeit likely upside down. He then managed to manoeuvre it up the steep hillside, sawing pieces out of fallen logs as he passed through and then returning the extracted pieces to cover his tracks. What he intended to do with the ATV at the camp is another mystery; it had to be airlifted out by Shuswap Search and Rescue after he vacated the camp. He also stole files from one cabin and attempted to extort the owner into providing him with enough cash for a computer. Most frighteningly for his neighbours on the Shuswap, he stole ten guns, which were found ominously positioned in a pit dug around his camp.

By spring he had become discouraged and returned to Calgary to earn some money and collect more information on missing children. He sensed he was unlikely to have any more run-ins with Bre-X thugs there; he suspected the men who had attacked him at his office resided elsewhere. At the same time, he was fearful of returning to his previous work, which would draw attention to him. Instead, he worked at a meat packing plant for a few months and stayed at a hostel while he earned enough to purchase a computer and other supplies. He also visited the Missing Children Society to collect information and pictures.

He then headed to the West Coast, stopping at the Shuswap for a couple of weeks on the way. In the Fraser Valley town of Langley he contacted an old girlfriend named Michelle, whom he had met in 1995 while he was hauling mining supplies to Williams Lake. On those trips, he would pull over at the Husky truck stop in Cache Creek, where Michelle, twenty-two at the time, was waiting tables. She had found him to be a sweet man, and they had started going on dates whenever he passed through. After he abruptly stopped calling, Michelle moved to Langley with her family.

When he reconnected with her by phone, he said he wasn't working anymore and had been hitchhiking around in search of work. He asked if he could visit her, and she agreed. He was at her door the next day. After that, he took her out for dinners and treated her and her friends to a concert. He even proposed to her, but she said she needed to finish college before deciding. In the meantime, Bjornstrom decided to hitchhike to Calgary to find work, and at seven o'clock one morning Michelle dropped him off at a Shell gas station in Langley.

Instead of catching a ride, he was spotted at the gas station by the RCMP on an outstanding arrest warrant in connection with the initial break-ins around the Shuswap. It's unclear how they stumbled upon him there. He left a backpack and duffel bag with Michelle, and she eventually opened them a couple of years later when they remained unretrieved and found clothing, income tax forms from 1997, an employment insurance benefits form showing $8,359 received that same year, business cards, a receipt for a post office box rental in Sorrento and another for one night's accommodation at a motel in Sicamous. The motel receipt was made out to his alias, William Sackett, a character in the western novels of Louis L'Amour. The fictional Sackett was a stoic man who kept to himself and took on various jobs that suited him as he drifted about and, although he was quick to fight like a "rabid wolf" if pushed, he abided by his father's rule: "Always ride on the side of the law, never against it."

Bjornstrom was sent to the Kamloops Regional Correctional Centre to await trial. He was given a psychiatric evaluation that stated his objective was to break into cabins to survive. "He denied having any intention to use the firearms in any type of violent manner," the report said, but he was "unclear as to why ten of the firearms were found in a loaded state in his base camp." According to Bjornstrom's self-assessment, he was stable and did not display any signs of a mood disorder, though he did believe he had a "sixth sense" that helped him predict the future but was not always accurate. The report ended by stating that "his thought processes were clear and well-organized."

He was sentenced to eight months, which began at the minimum-security Bear Creek Correctional Centre north of Kamloops, on the edge of Wells Gray Provincial Park. It was an open-air camp used to transition low-risk offenders back into society. The facilities included a sawmill and woodworking shop to manufacture items of benefit to the local community and adjacent park, and inmates were trained in skills such as firefighting. The centre had once housed cattle ranching and farming operations as well, which would have been a natural fit for Bjornstrom, but those facilities had been shut down in the 1980s, so he took a job baking.

He was later transferred to another open-air camp, the Rayleigh Correctional Centre on the outskirts of Kamloops. At times during its history, prisoners there had tended cattle and farmed and even canned vegetables in the on-site cannery and, in an especially random departure from what one imagines typical prison life to entail, made "concrete critters," lawn ornaments formed from molds and sold commercially. However, when Bjornstrom arrived, most of the open-air activities consisted of public service, such as cleaning garbage from highway ditches and maintaining hiking and ski trails in the area.

Bjornstrom seemed prepared to serve out his sentence at Rayleigh. He continued to communicate with Michelle, who intended to marry him once she finished college, and he told her that he planned to live in Langley when he had finished serving his time. His plans suddenly changed, though. According to Rob Nicholson, Bjornstrom said he was in the yard when he noticed two men get out of a pickup truck parked outside the prison yard fence. One of them was looking his way with binoculars, and then the other one pulled a rifle out of the vehicle and fired two quick shots in Bjornstrom's direction, one of them narrowly missing his head and lodging into the exterior of the prison wall. Although he had only six weeks remaining in his sentence, he panicked and decided it was time to flee to the Shuswap again. According to Bjornstrom, he found a spot in the fence line that he could crawl under and kept walking.

As he headed down the barren slope below the prison toward the train tracks along the river, he would have been easy to spot in his red prison garb—male inmates in BC wear red T-shirts, sweatshirts and pants, which they sew as part of a program to reduce costs and provide skill training. Fortunately for him, however, if more than one prison supervisor is available when an escape occurs, an escapee can be pursued to maintain line of sight, but capture can only take place after police assistance arrives. As he reached the tracks, a freight train was slowing down to a crawl, and he managed to get on the other side of it.

He headed back to the Shuswap, walking for three days on a route parallel to the South Thompson River, the outlet of the Shuswap Lake system and the 526 rivers and streams that feed it. His route detoured into the backcountry, moving from the semi-arid shrub steppe found in the Kamloops area, up through mixed forests of spruce, fir, pine, cedar and birch near the Sun Peaks ski resort, where in the sunny patches he was able to forage for late-maturing berries. He exited the woods at Little Shuswap Lake, an extension of the southwest arm of the Shuswap, and there he stole a canoe and paddled the roughly sixty kilometres to the far end of the lake, where he would begin excavating his cave.

SHUSWAP LAKE

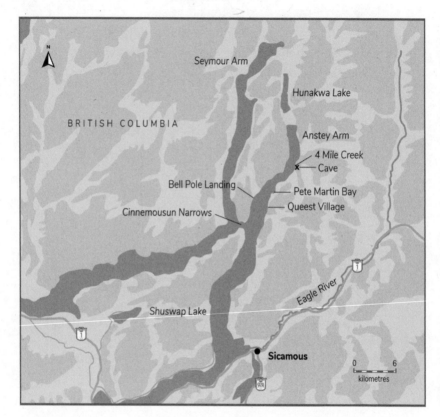

CHAPTER 10

SKOOKUM TUMTUM

> ❝ Unbelievable was my exact word when I looked down the tunnel. Nobody, but nobody, ever accused that man of being lazy."
>
> RCMP Sergeant **Jim Harrison**, describing Bjornstrom's cave

The word *skookum* sprouted from Chinook jargon, the simplified language developed in the nineteenth century to facilitate communication between groups of people trading in the Pacific Northwest who were otherwise mutually incomprehensible to one another. The word is typically understood to mean brave or strong. When combined with *tumtum*, which means to feel, think or hope, it means brave and good-hearted. It was a name bestowed upon geologist and surveyor George Dawson by a Secwépemc First Nations guide—and deservedly so.

Dawson travelled great distances throughout Canada's west and north and endured significant hardship to expand knowledge about the country's geology, geography, Indigenous cultures, botany and paleontology. Before he was even forty years old, he had surveyed 1,300 kilometres along the forty-ninth parallel for the British North American Boundary Commission, prepared comprehensive reports on many Indigenous peoples, named some of the Canadian Rockies' most iconic mountains, discovered rich coal seams that influenced the routing of the Canadian Pacific Railway, discovered dinosaur bones in Alberta and Saskatchewan, produced the first official survey of the Yukon and established the boundary between Yukon and Alaska. To complete the latter two tasks, Dawson undertook a four-month, two-thousand-kilometre journey by canoe.

Still, it took much more to become skookum tumtum than just enduring endless days of slogging along rough trails on horseback, dense bush on foot or tempestuous waters in a canoe while battling adverse weather and clouds of mosquitoes and blackflies, occasionally all at the same time. Rather it was his readiness to share all work and laugh at every obstacle that earned him rare praise from the Indigenous people he worked with. It was especially noteworthy because, whereas he may have been very skookum in nature, he was not skookum in physical well-being. At the age of eleven, he was afflicted by Pott's disease, a form of tuberculosis that softens and collapses the vertebrae. It left his spine twisted and curved, stunted his height at four-foot-six, and frequently debilitated him with severe migraines.

While exploring Shuswap, Dawson developed close relationships with the Secwépemc people, who had resided in the area for thousands of years. He provided a remarkably detailed account of their daily life, which he published as *Notes on the Shuswap People of British Columbia*. On his first trip, in 1877, he surveyed the region in a dugout canoe and encountered numerous Secwépemc people living in camps and subsisting on whitefish, kokanee and potatoes from their gardens while they waited for the next salmon run. It was Dawson who named the centre of the Shuswap H, a common meeting place for Indigenous groups, the Cinnemousun Narrows, which means "going around a point or bend." He travelled to the end of Anstey Arm and described a setting largely unchanged today: "The scenery wild and the sides rising steeply from the water for several miles toward the head with scarcely a vestige of beaches anywhere. Only a talus of great broken stones plunging down into dark, indigo water, with here and there a great tree trunk blown over by the wind and pointing to the depths below. One might well imagine oneself in one of the fjords of the Coast and indeed these lakes are nothing more."

He also observed that caves were important to the Secwépemc people and showed up in many of their stories. Nearly all the lakes in the area were believed to have hosted some form of monster at some point, and many of those monsters were cave dwellers. On his first trip he heard of the Shuswap Lake monsters, "water people" who were similar to mermaids or mermen but twice the size of humans. They possessed malign power that could create dangerous winds, and accordingly the Secwépemc people were apprehensive to pass too closely to their home in a cave below the water's surface at Copper Island, located at the end of the southwest Shuswap Arm, lest their canoes be swamped. That wasn't the only threat lurking at Copper Island; according to Secwépemc legend, it also housed a giant, human-eating bear named Ta Lana that at one time lived in a cave there.

On a subsequent trip a Secwépemc guide showed Dawson an entrance to a limestone cave in the Scotch Creek area near Copper Island that was too steep to enter without ropes, and alluded to a similar cave on nearby Squilax Mountain. According to locals, these caves have not been found since then, nor is the Shuswap region known for concealing many natural caves. Neither is it home to many abandoned mines, as mineralization is very limited in the region. The closest mine to Anstey Arm is the Iron Mask at Marble Point, north of Sicamous. By 1905, it employed seventy-three men, and they excavated a tunnel 220 feet long, but little information exists beyond that. The entrance to the main shaft can now be visited in one of the local marine parks.

While it is possible that undiscovered caves and mining tunnels exist in the region, locals familiar with the area are not aware of the existence of any *habitable* underground spaces. Bjornstrom's subterranean abode does not appear to have been an exception; that is, he didn't miraculously stumble upon a cave that was conveniently located near the water, was totally obscured from view and offered a sensible layout for a nine-hundred-square-foot bachelor pad. In interviews after he was arrested, he said he chose the location because of a "gut feeling that this was a place that they wouldn't be able to find me."

He said he spent five months carving out his cave with a hammer and chisel, then hauling the debris out in buckets and piling it where it would blend in with the surrounding terrain. When the tunnel reached thirty feet—enough to increase the temperature-moderating effects from the earth—he turned right and continued for another ten feet and then carved out a thirteen-by-thirteen-foot bedroom chamber, which he framed in with walls, a floor and a ceiling and covered with plastic sheeting to keep the moisture out. While he was chiselling out the cave, he would alternate between sleeping in a tent and other hideouts he had built around the lake. "I was even working on building a back door, but that day never came," he said.

Cave houses do exist throughout the world, though they're relatively rare in North America. A three-thousand-square-foot cave house carved into a granite hillside, recently listed for sale in Arizona, was created by specialists who took a year and a half of blasting to carve out the space and reinforce the ceiling with steel rods. It's always close to room temperature inside and water is supplied from a wall seep.

Anecdotal evidence of individuals carving out large volumes of rock by hand is harder to come by. In 1985 the wife of an Armenian villager named Levon Arkelian sent him below the family house to dig a hole to keep potatoes cool. He started excavating with a hammer and chisel and didn't stop for twenty-three years, working as much as eighteen hours a day as the rock "drew him in." At first progress was slow through solid black basalt, but he eventually broke through to "buttery volcanic stone" that was much easier to remove and allowed him to decorate the passages with ornate carvings in the walls. When he died in 2008, he had completed a roughly three-thousand-square-foot cave, now a museum operated by his wife.

Possibly the most extreme example of an individual carving through rock by hand is that of Dashrath Manjhi, a man in the Bihar region of India, who single-handedly carved a three-hundred-foot road through a mountain that isolated his village from the nearest town. He became determined after his wife was injured while trekking up a rocky footpath and they were forced to travel around the mountain to the nearest hospital; she subsequently died. To spare anyone else the same sorrow, he sold the family's three goats to purchase a hammer and chisels and, after plowing farmers' fields in the morning, worked on the road throughout the evenings and nights. After twenty-two years of toiling he completed the road, which had sides twenty-six feet high and was up to thirty feet wide.

While Bjornstrom's cave wasn't nearly as expansive, could he have carved it out in such a short time frame? Conveniently, Rob Nicholson was able to shed some light on the matter: before he became a private investigator, he served three of his five years in the military as a combat engineer with a unit in the Special Service Force, and followed that with twelve years as an explosives tech working on roads and other infrastructure projects throughout BC. He estimated it would have taken him at least six months of full-time work to carve out the Anstey Arm cave, and that would have been using small charges and a jackhammer instead of a hammer and chisel. Even if Bjornstrom had been able to get his hands on explosives, Nicholson feels he likely would have needed assistance to avoid killing himself.

Bjornstrom's cave no longer exists—it was imploded by the Ministry of Forests shortly after it was discovered—but remnants are still visible, so I was able to get some rock samples and asked a local geoscientist named Peter Weisinger for help identifying them. He has spent almost twenty years studying the geology of the area and was intrigued by the prospect of learning more about the Bushman's cave. He described the cave's location as "on the edge of the Shuswap metamorphic complex, which consists of an enigmatic mix of highly metamorphosed

Proterozoic rocks and more recent (i.e., Jurassic) intrusive rocks, with some sedimentary rocks in and around the granitic intrusions." He suspected, based on the samples I gave him, that it was most likely a sedimentary or metamorphic rock that was altered by the adjacent granitic intrusion and thereby made more workable.

In addition to the effort Bjornstrom put into carving the cave, he also went to great lengths to outfit it. From cabins on Pete Martin Bay, Bjornstrom took much of the lumber he used to install frames to support the tunnel ceiling, construct the bedroom walls, floor and ceiling, and build furniture such as the kitchen shelving, bed and closets. From cabins near Bell Pole Landing he took a small washing unit and a generator. He also took solar panels that he mounted in the trees on the hillside above the cave and connected to the battery bank inside.

He maintained his hygiene by bathing and showering. How exactly he did so came as a surprise to the RCMP officers who interviewed him after his arrest:

> Officer One: "You look very healthy. So you'd just
>   bathe in the lake and stuff?"
> Bjornstrom: "I had a hot tub."
> Officer One: "Hot tub?"
> Officer Two: "You have a hot tub?"

He had assembled it using a large barrel as the tub and a pump to circulate water through pipes and hoses, and warmed the water with a propane-fuelled heater. When the water reached a comfortable temperature, he removed the tub lid and submerged himself. The missing items that had puzzled one cabin owner were no longer a mystery: "After he took my water pump, he stole the jets out of my neighbour's hot tub. Then another guy lost a hose and another guy lost some pipes. I guess he put all that stuff together into something." For a shower, Bjornstrom used solar-heated water supplemented with water he boiled in a kettle. To further maintain good hygiene, he cut his hair short with scissors, thus minimizing the potential for things to live in it: "If you hunt a rabbit, for example, the lice that live in a rabbit's hair can also live in a human's hair," he told the RCMP.

For clothing he tended to rely on the fashion sense of one particular cabin owner, who noted that whenever he saw a newspaper photo of Bjornstrom, he was always wearing something from that man's closet: a green plaid jacket, a backpack, the Millarville Races shirt he was arrested in. More peculiar was seeing a Global News interview that showed a video of the Bushman riding the cabin owner's son's 80cc dirt bike, which he had somehow transported across the lake from near Bell Pole Landing.

He also collected guns in even greater numbers than during his first sojourn in the Shuswap. He often carried a .357 magnum handgun he had taken from a trapper's cabin and occasionally a sawed-off .22-calibre rifle or a pellet gun. His preferred choice for hunting small game such as grouse, rabbit and squirrel was the pellet gun because it was quiet and wouldn't disclose his location. At other times he opted for the slightly higher-calibre .22, from which he had removed the stock to make it easier to carry. He had other weapons stashed at his main camp and satellite camps. One startling acquisition he allegedly made was from a cabin in the Seymour Arm area, the northwest arm of the Shuswap. According to Bjornstrom, it was a long-barrel Uzi with a battery-powered night scope and about eight hundred rounds of nine-millimetre ammunition. He had also found an AK-47 in the same trapper's cabin from which he had appropriated the .357. He said he stole guns to hunt with or to defend himself if need be, and his explanation for stealing more of them than he needed was to prevent them being used against him. The RCMP were understandably concerned about the whereabouts of the guns when they eventually caught him, especially the assault weapons, but Bjornstrom was adamant they would never be found.

He said he only used the .357 handgun once, and that was when he was forced to shoot a cougar—a singular instance of killing a larger animal, something he otherwise refrained from, as he would be unable to avoid wasting the meat. The cougar charged him, and although he rebuffed it once with bear spray, it came at him again, so he shot it with the .357 and used as much of the meat as he could. Another run-in with a cougar occurred when he stumbled upon a deer that had fallen victim to one. He portioned off a hind quarter of the prey for himself, and when the predator returned and didn't appear interested in sharing its kill, he had to scare it away.

He avoided hunting close to his camp because he enjoyed having wildlife around. In one interview he explained that working with horses had given him a better sense of how to read animals, as horses get spooked when they sense fear in humans because it makes humans' actions more unpredictable. He translated that to the bush, arguing that wildlife also get spooked if they sense people are scared, and accordingly they prepare themselves for potential problems, which occasionally leads to aggressive behavior. He had numerous encounters with bears, including a sow and her cub that were grazing on the same crop of blueberries he was picking. When he inadvertently found himself between them, she swatted him across the face, leaving a cut near his eyebrow and across his chin. He washed up in the nearby creek and continued picking berries, though he kept a warier eye on the mama bear and a greater distance from her and her cub.

Another day, when he was cleaning up near a garden he had planted, a deer approached and rammed him lightly with its head. Slightly alarmed, he moved to his garden, but the deer approached him again. When he stepped back again, the deer tried to rub its head with its front leg. He sensed the deer was trying to communicate with him. Noticing some swelling behind its ear, he suspected the deer had a tick. He grabbed some Vaseline to try to suffocate the tick and force it to the surface, and the deer stood calmly while he applied it. Using Vaseline is not commonly recommended, as a tick has extremely low respiration rates of about four times per hour when resting, so smothering it with Vaseline is a more protracted solution than just pulling it out with tweezers. Nevertheless, he eventually removed a large tick. The deer lingered around his camp for a while afterwards, which he presumed was its way of giving thanks.

He fed himself by preparing the small game he hunted as a stew or stir-fry and by harvesting the carrots, lettuce, parsnips, peas and tomatoes he grew in a small greenhouse. In addition to picking blueberries, he also foraged for other types of berries, wild mushrooms and red clover, which he used for tea. When the opportunity arose, he fished, though usually away from

Shuswap Lake so that he was less likely to encounter anyone. He said he even ate a porcupine he came upon: "It's close to the taste of pork, but very difficult to skin."

He also established five satellite camps around the lake as stopover locations for his longer journeys or as surveillance points. These camps were tree stands thirty to eighty feet above the ground that he constructed by climbing the trees and hauling pre-drilled pieces of wood up with a rope. The height was selected to minimize the likelihood of animals disturbing them, give him a vantage point and make the camps less detectable from above, as they blended in with the tree canopy. They were typically accessed with a rope ladder and stockpiled with enough food to allow for a longer stay if necessary.

To replenish his supplies, he would sometimes venture farther afield, including to the end of Seymour Arm, about twelve kilometres, as the crow flies, from the end of Anstey Arm. It is only a shadow of the booming Seymour City it briefly became in the mid-1860s, when it supplied prospectors caught up in the Big Bend Gold Rush on the Upper Columbia River. The boom times did not last long, however, as the remaining gold was proving prohibitive to extract, and the port of Seymour Arm that was established to receive prospectors arriving by sternwheeler was shut down one year after opening.

Various attempts at industry have spurted to life in the intervening years—orchards, forestry, marijuana—but today the permanent population of about eighty people relies mainly on tourism during the summer months, when the population increases up to six-fold. The only store now is Daniels Store and Marina, opened in 1963 by a local named Alf Daniels. His grandparents settled in what became known as Daniels Bay in 1908, travelling there from Sicamous with all their possessions in a rowboat while pulling a barge carrying two horses. Alf Daniels started his store in a small shack on the shore and, when business increased, towed a former floating restaurant to Daniels Bay and converted it into a larger store. Perhaps Bjornstrom was off the radar on Seymour Arm, as he apparently slipped in and out of the store undetected.

Three or four times a year, he also travelled by canoe to Sicamous, the closest town by water to his cave. Designated the Houseboat Capital of Canada, Sicamous is the staging point for all the houseboats on Shuswap Lake. Given that travelling there was a serious undertaking, he tried to make it worthwhile. On one occasion he took along a particularly large harvest of blueberries and sold it to a fruit stand vendor for a couple of hundred dollars.

There was a closer shopping option: two floating stores at the Cinnemousun Narrows cater to houseboaters travelling from one arm to the other as well as revellers already in need of replenishing their fluids after their initial three-hour journey from Sicamous. Both stores sit on floating barges and carry a wide selection of merchandise, including an assortment of costumes for the rowdy parties at Nielsen Beach on Seymour Arm. These stores were presumably avoided by Bjornstrom, though, as he would have been very conspicuous pulling alongside in a canoe. And clearly convenience was not of paramount importance to him, as the furthest he ventured by foot for a meal was over the Monashee Mountains to Revelstoke (a two-hour drive by car from Anstey Arm) to celebrate his birthday by enjoying a Big Mac among the highway travellers. "Something different than eating squirrels," he said.

To supplement what he could hunt, gather, grow and purchase, he also helped himself to food he could scavenge from nearby cabins, particularly dry goods left for the winter. One cabin owner who had left food in his freezer arrived at his place by snowmobile in midwinter and surprised Bjornstrom, who was inside cooking a hamburger. Bjornstrom, who quickly fled through the snow, was likely aware that this particular cabin was regularly used during the winter months and so would be stocked with food, as opposed to the summer cabins, which would be cleared out, but it was a daring move—it would have been easy to track him in the snow.

He took a hodgepodge of small items from most cabins, and several owners were content with helping him get by, one owner estimating the value of the goods taken to be less than what would disappear from his wallet in one night at a bar with friends. Some cabin owners, concerned that he would damage their cabins while trying to gain entry, would leave food and other supplies out for him: a few cans of food, a bar of soap, toilet paper, things left over from the summer. He would often leave a note in return saying how grateful he was not to have to break in. Or if someone else had broken into the cabin, he would leave a note with the date of his visit and a description of the condition in which he found the place before he fixed what he could.

He attempted to prod other cabin owners into leaving food and supplies for him—outright extortion, he later acknowledged—by leaving cassette tape messages or notes suggesting he would avoid breaking into their cabins if they left supplies. In more prescriptive messages, he specified that food should be sealed in plastic containers and gasoline put in jerry cans. He also noted that empty containers would later be returned and, upon request, he would provide receipts for any received goods for a deemed amount. He then signed off, occasionally with a benediction of some sort. "Well, you and your family have a great summer and safe boating" was the sign-off at the end of one rambling tape-recorded message.

To elicit insight from cabin owners regarding their interactions with Bjornstrom, I set out by kayak in an attempt to catch folks by the water. Arriving during a summer evening, I found a couple of inviting beaches and picked one to set up my camp for the night while a houseboat settled into the other. I passed the evening marvelling at the idyllic setting and enjoying the tranquility. With nothing to do, however, I retired early, hoping to enjoy a full slumber. The first noise that shook the tent was the roar from the souped-up engine of a boat going back and forth across the arm. I wondered if perhaps the driver was trying to scare away visitors like myself. Then, just as the initial clamor subsided, the beat dropped next door, where the houseboaters were ramping up their party. I wallowed in the cacophony for a while before sleep came—fractionally.

Early the next morning, with serenity restored, I paddled toward the floating stores to confirm they had no recollection of Bjornstrom ever making any purchases. Realizing they weren't open yet, I paddled back toward the cabins to wait for any occupants to emerge. As I passed the previously thumping houseboat, expecting it to be dormant, I was surprised to see a woman launching herself down the slide at the rear of the boat. Her face held far more surprise than mine, though, as she clearly hadn't seen me approaching and had forsaken her swimsuit.

Gradual signs of life emerged as I reached the clusters of rustic, off-the-grid cabins near Bell Pole Landing, which are inviting and aloof at the same time. I was taking my time trying to find someone to approach—and simultaneously mustering the courage to intrude upon the vacationers' pleasant morning—when I noticed a lady walking along the shoreline between cabins. She appeared to be collecting debris that had washed up on the shore, and I gradually approached. Then, just as I was struggling with my opening line, a black bear emerged from the woods close by. I seized the opportunity.

"Excuse me, ma'am. Just wanted to let you know there's a black bear walking along the shore a couple of hundred feet away. I'm sure you see them all the time, but just thought I'd let you know."

"Well actually, we don't see them that often, so thanks." She quickly started back toward the cluster of cabins she had come from, skipping over some debris in the process as she hastened her pace.

"Sorry to bother you," I said as I paddled alongside her, "but I'm doing some research for a potential book on the Bushman and was wondering if you might have any thoughts on him."

"Oh, he wasn't very well liked around here."

Her family had just bought their cabin when Bjornstrom began targeting the area. The small clothes washer found in his cave came from their cabin, along with a generator. What most disturbed her, though, was his letters. One of the more unnerving ones read: "I saw your kids waterskiing, and it looks like they're improving." She told me that her neighbours a few doors down found a note stating: "It looks like you have a nice family and I like your dogs."

The neighbours were indeed a nice family and allowed me to intrude upon their breakfast. They referred to their cabin as the Bushman's Canadian Tire and had reverted to leaving the door open to accommodate him. Feeling they had already lost plenty, they were surprised to find a note one day stating that if a Rubbermaid container filled with dry goods wasn't left for him, "you may not have a cabin to come back to in the spring." Bjornstrom later made an apparent attempt at repentance: on their dock, the owners found two rifles that had been stolen from them, with a note reading: "I can be a nice guy. Can you please phone NL Radio in Kamloops and tell them?"

They told me another neighbour arrived one spring to find a note in a bottle from Bjornstrom, indicating he had spent time there during the winter and gone through their files. The note alleged that income tax returns found in the cabin did not align with the investment portfolio statements he had also found there. Furthermore, after going through the gardening books on their shelves, he speculated that the owner was growing marijuana. The note concluded by threatening that if they didn't leave $200 and ten gallons of gasoline for him, he was going to the RCMP with his findings.

Of all the items he stole, the most astounding might be the wood stove that weighed over two hundred pounds, along with the accompanying stovepipe. It had been an undertaking for the owner and his son to move it into the cabin on Pete Martin Bay, where Bjornstrom found it awaiting installation, yet Bjornstrom somehow managed to move it himself, transport it up the lake and haul it up to his cave, where it again awaited installation before the RCMP removed it.

To start his journeys at nightfall, he must have first extricated his canoe from the bottom of the lake. Then a one-way journey from his cave to the marked cabin would likely have taken him roughly an hour and a half. The return trip would be more sluggish with the added cargo, albeit only about twelve minutes longer in the case of the wood stove, assuming a rule-of-thumb loss of speed equivalent to one-sixth the percentage increase in mass, according to websites that estimate such things. He would then have to hump the items up the steep trail to his lair. Finally, he would have to re-submerge his canoe, tipping it on its side and filling it with rocks.

To see what the procedure of sinking a canoe necessitated, I enlisted the eager help of my kids to scupper our sixteen-footer. Filling it with water took a matter of seconds, but it still floated superficially. It took roughly the same weight in rocks as the canoe itself, about fifty-five pounds, to firmly lay it to rest on the bottom of the lake. The aluminum gunwale was still very visible in waist-deep water, though, which likely explains why Bjornstrom painted his canoes black.

I did not try paddling with anything like a wood stove, but such exertion in a canoe is certainly not unprecedented. David Thompson, one of the most prodigious of paddlers—who never actually made it to the Shuswap despite being the namesake of the river draining it—travelled over ninety thousand kilometres, mostly by canoe, while mapping a relatively large portion of North America. The five-man canoes he travelled in were laden with up to nearly three thousand pounds of cargo, nearly six hundred pounds per man. That's not to suggest Bjornstrom's misbegotten efforts to haul a stolen wood stove up the lake were otherwise comparable to Thompson's valiant undertakings. Still, it must have been a daunting feat in the dark by himself.

What was doubly perplexing though, was that in his interview with the RCMP after his arrest, he referred to another wood stove located in an underground hideout on an altogether different lake. At the end of Anstey Arm, an old trail follows a creek into the Anstey Hunakwa Provincial Park to the isolated body of water known as Hunakwa Lake. It was near that lake that Bjornstrom allegedly established his other camp: a wood-and-stone structure measuring about thirteen by sixteen feet. He claimed it was built above ground against a hillside and covered with over two feet of earth and rock. The door was made of wood and masonry and covered with moss. The wood stove was located inside and vented by forty feet of stovepipe that extended up the hillside, where it was buried under about two feet of earth. Small holes along the stovepipe dissipated smoke through the rocks and moss so that it was not released through a single, potentially revealing source. He would lift the moss along the forest floor when he arrived and replace it when he left so there was no trail. It would be impossible to find, he said. In a Global News interview he gave from prison, he said it contained a bag of videotapes he had discovered in a cabin, one of which showed children being sexually abused at a cabin in the area. He asked that this tape be taken to the Missing Children Society, not the RCMP: "It will give more insight as to why I was really there."

CHAPTER 11

HUNAKWA

> ❝ I've gone a little bit overboard on some things."
> **John Bjornstrom**

When RCMP officers from the Kamloops District Major Crime Unit interviewed Bjornstrom after his arrest—a pleasant diversion from their typical investigations, they acknowledged—they tried to coerce him into disclosing the location of his hideout on Hunakwa Lake. "If I give you everything, then I have nothing," he countered. They argued that safety was a concern if firearms were stashed there; they didn't want to risk the weapons falling into the wrong hands. Bjornstrom reassured them that he had camouflaged it extremely well to avoid such an outcome. Still they persisted.

"What if another resourceful person comes along?" they asked. "They're going to find it."

"You have to know where it is to see it," he maintained. "It has two feet of earth on top of it and it's surrounded by over two feet of earth as well. You can look at it and you won't see it."

"Sounds like it's up that quad trail, I'm just guessing," suggested one of the officers.

"There is no trail."

"Where that creek runs down there."

"There is no trail."

"Little trail with a creek running down on the north side."

"There are many, many creeks out there."

But Bjornstrom did provide some details in that RCMP interview that gave clues to its location. He told them he would hike the trail from Anstey Arm and then canoe to his camp on Hunakwa. He said the structure was roughly thirteen by sixteen feet and the stovepipe extended about forty feet up the hillside under two feet of earth, so it was presumably located at the toe of a steep slope.

It's possible he used explosives to create it. He did have some familiarity with explosives from his trucking days, and he testified at his trial that he had taken explosives from cabins—including a type of dynamite called Geogel, used for seismic work, as well as explosives used for road construction. However, he also explained, he had used only a chisel and hammer to carve out the less remote Anstey Arm cave.

The Hunakwa camp must have been located close to a creek, as he generated electricity with a micro hydro generator. And given that he was picking up moss and replacing it to avoid leaving a trail, the location was likely not too far from the lakeshore.

"I'm truly looking forward to seeing this," said one of the officers.

"Well, you've got a challenge."

"Well, don't underestimate our guys."

"No, I don't underestimate 'em, but . . . uh . . . don't underestimate me either."

According to Sergeant Jim Harrison, the RCMP never bothered to look for the hidden lair—a sensible decision given the description they had received. And after nearly two decades of believing the cave had been his principal lair and witnessing the effort that had gone into its construction, I didn't think I would look for it either. It was almost unfathomable to me that he could have established a second home on an entirely different lake farther north. But the various accounts he gave were tough to ignore. I had wanted to visit Hunakwa Lake anyway, and the lair's description evoked images from books I had read as a kid—something akin to Mr. Tumnus's Narnian abode, complete with a wood stove.

It was already fall when I concluded a trip was warranted, so there wasn't much time to do it. I would need a team. Conveniently, one of my friends was the ideal candidate: let's call him Manders. He's been a go-to companion in the outdoors for a few decades and continually surprises with his wide-ranging wilderness knowledge, the source of much of it unknown to me. He had been in the cave on Anstey Arm with me back in 2002, so he too had a lingering curiosity regarding the Bushman. I had a feeling he would relish the challenge and enjoy the trip regardless of the outcome. It took no convincing. He was in.

The third member of the team was more unexpected. I was speaking with my parents on the phone—conference calls being a preferred method of communication after many years of one or the other interjecting from the background—and filling them in on my plans.

"I'm in," my father said.

"Pardon?" my mother and I said in unison.

"I'll come with you."

My father's always been a good sport, game for pretty much anything, but his interest in such a half-baked undertaking caught me off guard. "It could take a lot of paddling to get to the end of Anstey Arm," I cautioned.

"Great."

We'd been on paddling trips before, so I had no concerns about whether he could handle that part. Searching for something elusive wasn't that far-fetched for him either, as he too had sought out the Bushman's cave in 2002, with another group. And even more tellingly, just the previous week he had ventured off into the woods with a group looking for wild horses, of all things, and had continued for five hours of bushwhacking. So the team was set.

We would take the logging road over Queest Mountain, leave a vehicle at an acquaintance's cabin and paddle to the end of Anstey Arm. (A motorized boat was considered, but that would have been less skookum.) We would camp overnight at the end of Anstey and portage to Hunakwa Lake the next day to explore. My map showed eight creeks flowing into the south end of Hunakwa, and we would start with the larger ones.

Before setting off, I decided to check with Rob Nicholson to see if he had any clues to divulge. In a previous conversation he had given me the impression he had some information he wasn't comfortable disclosing, but I thought it was worthwhile double-checking. This time he replied without hesitation: "John said it was a thousand yards up the lake on the west side." But he cautioned that once, when he had looked for something in the bush on Bjornstrom's behalf, he had found his distances to be off. Still, the new information changed everything. I started to believe we had a decent chance of finding the lair.

We set off paddling on glassy water on a tranquil fall day, my father and I in a canoe laden with gear, and Manders in a kayak. For me, long-distance paddling can be lulling and refreshingly novel, at least at first. It gets more daunting as the estimated number of remaining paddle strokes increases exponentially. Such was the case on this occasion, but it was also more invigorating than usual.

About halfway up Anstey Arm we made a stop to look for the trail up to Bjornstrom's cave. It was partly a challenge to see if we could still find it and partly to confirm its present condition. Having all seen it previously, we were perhaps over-confident in our ability to find it again. We scoured the relatively uniform shoreline, trying to spot the smallest detail that might trigger some memory, but everywhere the rocky banks led to what looked, from the water at least, like impenetrably steep and densely forested hillside. We couldn't find any hint of a trail leading farther up.

Humbled, we set off again, hoping for greater success with our principal mission. After roughly three hours of paddling we reached the end of the arm, and Manders, who was in the lead, began looking for a nice spot to camp on the beach adjacent to the creek flowing from Hunakwa. "We can't camp here," he reported back. "There are salmon skeletons and bear and wolf prints everywhere." Another attribute that makes Manders a great wilderness travelling companion is his alertness to danger—and judging by the smell from the water, the fall salmon run was indeed underway. "Let's look on the other end of the beach, where it probably smells less like death," he suggested.

The other end had picnic tables and outhouses, and we set up camp there, each of us with his own shelter. Manders had opted for a bivouac bag, the kind used by climbers forced to spend the night in tight spaces. From his perspective, the efficiency of travelling with his casket-like shelter more than compensated for its "suffocatingness."

Having encamped, we tried unsuccessfully to locate the start of the trail to Hunakwa and finally settled around the fire for the evening. When my kids were younger and didn't possess enough mental stamina for long hikes, I would distract them by telling them stories about Manders. They now request the stories on most hiking trips, and I've come to appreciate the tales' message, as they typically entail Manders overcoming adversity, misfortune regularly testing his mettle. Hearing the stories firsthand is optimal, however, and as I listened along I wondered if the following day would replenish my inventory.

As we retired to our shelters, Manders acknowledged that my father and I could probably sleep comfortably knowing that any visiting animals would be most attracted to him, in his minimalist bivy bag. I didn't hear any animal noises in the night, which is not to say that snorting bear-like sounds didn't emanate from either tent. But apparently Manders did, and being the fine wilderness companion he is, he undertook a middle-of-the-night patrol of the general area. The next morning, after varying degrees of rest, we were successful in finding the trail on the other side of the arm and set off towards Hunakwa with the intention of returning for the canoe if the trail would allow.

None of us expected more than plodding along a nondescript trail through the woods, so we were surprised by the verdant oasis that greeted us, drawing us farther into the forest. Its enchanting spell distracted us from thoughts of the canoe we planned to carry (Manders was not as easily sidetracked and sprinted ahead to see if by chance a boat had been left at the other end of the trail). The path beckoned through majestic western red cedars that monopolized the canopy above. Devil's club, native to damper, mountainous areas west of the Continental Divide, blanketed the forest floor below. On one side a mossy slope rolled along, and on the other the perfectly sedating Hunakwa Creek meandered.

Our destination was also well guarded. The trail detoured around several blow-down areas where old-growth trees of weighty girth lay at rest. Some had been uprooted, leaving large sections of the forest floor bare and the root system towering overhead. In other cases, the trees had been snapped off partway up, leaving splintered cedar to navigate around. It appeared as if an inordinately fierce windstorm had laid siege, though I later learned that a tree's girth isn't actually correlated with the wind speed required to topple it, nor is the height or species. When the trail didn't lead over, around or even under fallen cedars, it took us through muddy bogs that required us to balance perilously over unsteady detritus exposed just above the surface. This was preferable to detouring through the pervasive devil's club, though. Almost the entire plant—from its stems, which reach several feet in height, to its broad, maple-shaped leaves—is covered with slender thorns that break off upon contact and can take over a week to re-emerge from below the skin of an unwary passerby. Entire sections of the Canadian Pacific Railway had to be altered because workers found the devil's club too trying to work in. The canoe would not be joining us.

It was inconceivable how Bjornstrom could have hauled the materials for his Hunakwa home along the trail, but he had not been the only one to establish a camp on the lake. According to

George Dawson's notes from his initial visit, the Secwépemc people had somehow navigated up the creek in small canoes, a route that now appears impassable given the obstacles we observed.

One of the first settlers in the Shuswap region had also spent time in the Hunakwa area. Francis Anstey was an indomitable woodsman who usually worked alone. His name was bestowed on Anstey Arm after he assisted Dawson with explorations of the area. The two made a distinct pair, with the giant Anstey a full two feet taller. From 1875 to 1885 Anstey contracted with a mill in Kamloops to supply logs, but he also cut his own shingles, shakes and fencing, which he sold directly by advertising in a local paper: "All hand-made and of the finest and clearest cedar timber in the world. Infinitely superior to any machine-made roofing. The quality will suit the most fastidious, and the prices, everybody." A party exploring the Hunakwa area in 1906 discovered the remains of one of his trolley lines; the track, ties and car were all made of wood.

Anstey's fortitude was displayed toward the end of his life when he became acquainted with the perils of travelling the lake alone in a fully laden canoe. Near the Cinnemousun Narrows, he was surprised by a squall that overtook him and deposited him on a rocky shore. He managed to hold on to his Peterborough canoe but lost everything else. Two days later he reached the narrows, paddleless, having propelled his canoe five kilometres by other means. He was found there by searchers who had received word he had been lost in the storm.

Aside from intrepid explorers, Hunakwa does not generally see many visitors, which must have been part of its attraction for Bjornstrom. He could go fishing there in the daytime, especially if the cloud cover was low. There isn't a gradual transition from land to lake; the dense forest flares out over an abrupt shoreline. Bushwhacking along the steep slopes surrounding the lake is not impossible, but certainly proved wearisome in our case. The footing was uncertain, as the mossy carpet sometimes masked fragile ground below. We had to climb very carefully over large fallen trees greased up by the recent rains, and our route was often directed by dense thickets of chokecherry shrubs and fir boughs, which occasionally forced us onto our knees. One massive blowdown area was totally unnavigable and sent us far up the slope to bypass it. And the whole time we had to remain fixated on locating something specifically designed, nearly two decades earlier, to be impossible to find.

Manders led the charge, circulating up and down the slopes at a vigorous pace; my father travelled more cautiously, intent on avoiding a nasty slip. I focused my attention on the lower slopes, as it was hard to imagine Bjornstrom locating his camp very high above the lake; then again, I was basing that on what I would do, an increasingly dubious basis for guessing what the Bushman would have done.

A few creeks had seemingly attractive nooks for constructing a lair, but we found nothing. Indeed, there were almost no signs of human activity at all. The only exceptions were several culturally modified trees, likely carved by the Secwépemc people hundreds of years ago. The most obvious examples were western red cedars that had rectangular scars with cut and chop marks at top and bottom. The slabs of thick outer bark taken from these trees were typically used as roofing, wall lining and flooring for the pit or *kekuli* houses in which the Secwépemc people wintered. With the help of the whole village, one house could be constructed in a single day. Ideally, the sites chosen had a southern exposure, shelter from the wind, a dry sandy or gravelly soil and convenient access to water. Size depended on how many families were to reside within; the houses were built up to twenty-five feet in diameter and six feet below ground level. Dawson described the structures as radial "fascine," a framework made of bundles of small sticks and brush angled toward the centre, supported by larger posts and bound together using wet rawhide that would tighten and secure the structure as it dried. The roof was made from a combination of bark strippings and soil collected from excavating the site. Plants were grown in the roof soil to absorb moisture.

Pit houses didn't sound altogether different from Bjornstrom's description of his Hunakwa structure. Something that size could be camouflaged, but surely we couldn't have overlooked it in our exhaustive search. So, as we made our way back, we completed another thorough inspection across the slopes. We arrived back at Anstey Arm scraped, bruised and deflated to see fresh bear tracks—Manders discovered them first, of course, and duly alerted us—and the water exiting the creek speckled with more dead salmon.

"At least we're not salmon," Manders said as we navigated through their floating remains and contemplated the remarkable journey they had completed.

Sockeye salmon operate on a four-year cycle, and this happened to be a dominant year in that cycle. Their journey begins as tiny alevins in the gravel farther upstream. Only about 10 per cent of them survive freezing, overexposure to light, drying up from loss of water flow, getting stuck in excessive gravel or silt, or being gobbled up by predators. Downstream, freshwater fish, ducks and loons devour another three-quarters of those that make it into the Shuswap before they undergo body chemistry changes to allow them to live in salt water. After a couple of years navigating the ocean and avoiding a whole new set of predators—sharks, sea lions, seals, killer whales, dolphins and other fish—they somehow find their way upstream the river that delivered them while navigating yet more obstacles: predators, waterfalls, fish ladders, anglers, lice from fish farms, landslides and heart failure if the water is too warm. And as soon as they re-contact the fresh water, they stop eating and start dying. For each spent salmon floating upside down in the water we canoed through, roughly a thousand had started the journey in the creek bed upstream.

With the salmons' harrowing journey in mind, we had a little extra pluck in our paddle strokes as we set out across Anstey Arm. To remain on schedule, we elected to camp halfway back at Four Mile Creek, close enough to the location of Bjornstrom's cave that I felt compelled to make one more attempt to find it before dusk arrived.

I'm surprised I did. From the rocky shore there was absolutely no indication of its whereabouts, and the only tip-off was a slope that wasn't prohibitively steep and overgrown. In the middle of that slope was a faint trail barely discernible below the foliage. I followed the trail up a couple of still-navigable switchbacks to a pile of rubble overlain by fallen trees and strategically placed logs, a site that would be undetectable to anyone unaware of what had existed there previously. The only evidence of human presence was a few cans and plastic bottles.

When the RCMP cleared out the cave after it was discovered, it took seven of them a full day to remove the stolen property and shuttle it down the steep trail onto a barge. "It was tons of stuff," said Sergeant Harrison. "My back could tell you that." The cabin owners didn't bother retrieving any of it, though. By that point, according to one of them, "it wasn't worth a plugged nickel."

Harrison was concerned with the safety of visitors to the cave in the event a portion or all of it collapsed; it had begun to attract an increasing number of visitors, and some business owners in Sicamous were enthusiastic about making it a draw. "I'd like to turn it into a tourist attraction," announced the eager manager of one houseboat rental business. "It's the biggest thing in BC and to destroy it would be a waste." He planned to apply for a business licence to escort visitors to the site, and sought a court injunction to prohibit the RCMP from destroying it.

His comment on the tourism potential was perhaps a tad overzealous, but the cave was certain to attract more visitors. That's what happened to the abandoned bus in which Chris McCandless, the subject of Jon Krakauer's book *Into the Wild*, starved to death: it became a focal point of those following in the footsteps of the philosophizing traveller, despite the marathon trek across Alaskan tundra and the dangerous river crossing required to access it. Local authorities regularly had to rescue "pilgrims," as they became known, and on two occasions retrieved their bodies from the river. Local authorities finally removed the bus by helicopter in June 2020.

Trying to act pre-emptively in the interest of public safety, Harrison approached his superiors after clearing out much of the cave to seek permission to implode it. They didn't believe it should be an RCMP decision, so the task was instead handed over to the Ministry of Forests, which had it demolished.

Back at the campground, we enjoyed another pleasant evening around the fire, where Manders dried his shoes out from the day's muddy adventure and managed to melt only part of the rubber. Just as we were reflecting on how surprising it was that he hadn't suffered any setbacks on the trip, he spilled a full cup of hot cider on the shoes he had just dried.

Bjornstrom had said his lair was about a thousand yards from the end of the lake on the west side, but we bushwhacked maybe 1,700 yards along the western edge of the lake without finding it. Perhaps that hadn't been far enough. Nicholson later concurred; when Bjornstrom gave him instructions to retrieve some property, the distance to its location had ended up being about three times Bjornstrom's estimate. I could see on my map that about 2,500 yards up the west side of the lake was what appeared to be the largest stream entering the lake, draining a pond at the top of the ridge above it. Assuming Bjornstrom had installed a micro hydro generator as he suggested—one had indeed gone missing from a lakeside cabin but was never found at his cave—I became convinced that this was the location of the lair.

We would have to wait until the spring for a second attempt, and this time I would recruit some local help. The first person to come to mind was Jim Cooperman, the author of *Everything Shuswap: A Geographic Handbook*, a wide-ranging and wonderful tribute to *nearly* everything about the Shuswap—somehow two more volumes are to follow—that represents the culmination of twelve years of research. As if writing the book was not enough, Cooperman has arranged for all the proceeds to go toward enhancing the local school district's outdoor learning program. He arrived in the area from the US fifty years ago, during the Vietnam War, bought some land near the southwest tip of Shuswap Lake and hasn't moved since.

He had already been providing me with information on the Shuswap when I proposed he join us, and he didn't need much convincing, acknowledging he's never been one to turn down an adventure. He suggested that this time we go into the area from the north, through the settlement of Seymour Arm, and from there we could drive all the way to the lake on a little-known road. I gathered the team together again—thankfully they too were keen for another attempt—and we set off in early May. The forecast did not look attractive for camping, so I sought out a place to stay in Seymour Arm and stumbled upon a couple renting out rooms in their house. We showed up to find an unfinished building, the house wrap painted with bucolic vignettes.

Leeann, the laidback owner, directed us around the back, where we found a welcoming entrance to the off-the-grid Long Ridge Lodge and a splendid apartment where we would each have our own comfortable room. Our dinner, she told us, was staying warm. It was a truly unforgettable meal, especially considering it takes Leeann pretty much a full day just to shop for groceries. The next morning Cooperman showed up early to meet us at the lodge and was able to help us tackle another memorable meal. After he autographed Leeann's copy of *Everything Shuswap* and we expressed our supreme gratitude to our hostess, we headed out to encounter whatever lay ahead.

The road to the lake had been bulldozed through the forest in the 1960s to access a forest fire adjacent to the lake, but it clearly hadn't been travelled by vehicles in a long while: about fifty fallen trees blocked our path. Cooperman was able to use his small electric chainsaw to clear the first ones, but they grew greater and greater in girth, and we had to rely on the larger chainsaw that the ever-vigilant Manders had brought along.

Eventually we caught sight of the lake ahead, and it wasn't a moment too soon: the final behemoth blocking the road was far too big to cede to Manders's saw. What was supposed to have been a half-hour journey to the lake had taken four times longer, but now only a minor portage and a four-kilometre paddle on serene water remained. The trip required no exertion on my part; somehow I found myself in the middle of a canoe between two septuagenarian paddlers, while Manders dutifully probed ahead in his kayak. As the others paddled and a nearby loon wailed, I took in the views of the undisturbed forest surrounding the lake, which is home to old-growth cedar, hemlock and spruce, some over a thousand years old. Inland rainforests like this are unique in the world, existing only in select parts of southeastern British Columbia.

In the 1990s the area surrounding Hunakwa had been destined for logging, but the Shuswap Environmental Action Society (SEAS), led by Cooperman, rallied public support to protect it. Its efforts included several trips to the area to inventory the abundant fauna and flora, and for that purpose they hid a canoe under a log at the lake's south end. When the canoe later went missing, Cooperman assumed it had become part of Bjornstrom's fleet, but he isn't fussed about it: "It only cost a hundred dollars and served us well when we needed it. So not a big deal." I asked him what it's like to know he played a large part in protecting this jewel, and he said, "I love Hunakwa. I just wish more people could experience it, people who would appreciate it, and not those who would cause damage."

SEAS faced strong resistance. One of the first meetings regarding the fate of the area took place in Seymour Arm, a three-hour drive in a blinding snowstorm for Cooperman from his home at the other end of the lake. He knew many of the local residents and felt they were like-minded, but when they arrived at the meeting, they discovered that the logging company planning on clear-cutting the area had stacked the room with its employees. "Their goal was to intimidate the residents so that they wouldn't speak up," said Cooperman. "It didn't intimidate me."

At the time he was also chairman of another local organization called the Mara Shuswap Property Owners Society that advocated for more parks and worked collaboratively to keep clear-cutting away from watersheds and viewsheds. Its next meeting was also stacked with the employees of the same logging company. After putting down twenty dollars apiece for memberships and asking for receipts, they voted in a board of directors consisting entirely of their co-workers. It was the society's final meeting.

However, after toiling tirelessly for a decade to save the area around Hunakwa, SEAS members were delighted when the BC government announced the creation of the park in 2000. At the time Cooperman hoped funds could be raised to build a trail from Hunakwa over the ridge above—past Wright Lake on the other side and down to Seymour Arm to provide a wilderness opportunity for boaters—but it didn't happen.

The Hunakwa end of the proposed trail happened to be where we anticipated finding the Bushman's other lair, and it certainly seemed like the logical spot as we kicked off our search. It was also idyllic, with a cascading waterfall cloistered among velvety green moss feeding a meandering creek that flowed along the base of a gentle slope. Alas, no vestige of Bjornstrom's home could be found. After two decades, his already camouflaged lair is now probably indistinguishable from the landscape surrounding it. Or it could be in a different location. Or perhaps it never existed.

CHAPTER 12

OFF THE BEATEN TRACK

> ❝ I may seem like I'm off the beaten track most of the time, but I know what I'm doing 100 per cent of the time."
>
> John Bjornstrom

Christopher Knight, who became known as the North Pond Hermit, was twenty years old when he drove to a remote area of Maine, abandoned his car with the keys on the centre console and walked into the woods with just a tent and a backpack. Later he recalled that news of the Chernobyl disaster was on his car radio, which would make it 1986. He tried various dwellings, including a cave he dug out of a riverbank, before establishing a camp in a spot obscured by glacial erratic boulders and a thicket of hemlocks. It would be his home for the next twenty-seven years while he survived off supplies he stole from nearby cabins and camps.

Knight's hermitage was recounted in Michael Finkel's book *The Stranger in the Woods*. According to Finkel, Knight had just two encounters with other people during that twenty-seven-year period: a "hi" exchanged with a hiker on a trail in the 1990s and an encounter with a family of fishermen—grandfather, father and son—who discovered his camp and agreed not to disclose the encounter to police. Describing the solitude, Knight said: "I lost my identity. With no audience, no one to perform for, I was just there. There was no need to define myself; I became irrelevant. The moon was the minute hand, the seasons the hour hand. I didn't even have a name. I never felt lonely. To put it romantically, I was completely free."

His first intention had been to live off the land, though it wasn't a particularly well devised plan, as foraging for food in Maine—where, as Finkel puts it, "some berry seasons last a weekend"—is extremely difficult. One would have to be highly proficient at hunting, trapping and/or fishing to exist by those means alone, and even though Knight was an experienced hunter and fisherman, he had neither a gun nor a rod and was trying to conceal his presence. After attempts at foraging, including a distasteful sampling of road-killed partridge, had thwarted him for long enough, his scruples wore down sufficiently that he began to steal. He committed about forty burglaries per year, eventually reaching over one thousand in total.

There are rare instances of hunter-gatherers still roaming parts of North America, living as humans have lived for 99 per cent of our history. For example, the Coyote Camp people travel throughout the southwestern US, guided by the harvest times of edible plants and replacing the plants they harvest with new seeds. Generally, however, the skills and knowledge required to subsist solely on hunting and gathering have been lost. The most well-known example of a modern-day attempt may be that of Chris McCandless and his plan to live off the land in Alaska for a summer, a venture that ended in starvation. It's taken a couple of decades to resolve exactly what led to his death, illustrating the difficulty of trying to replicate the wealth of hunter-gatherer knowledge built up over thousands of years of trial and error. (*Into the Wild* author Jon Krakauer assembled a team of scientists who confirmed in 2015 that McCandless inadvertently poisoned himself by consuming a large volume of wild potato seeds—the book had just blamed the wrong toxin in the seeds—and cautions other foragers that even when some parts of a plant are known to be edible, other parts may be toxic.)

McCandless, like many others who undertake to live directly off the land, took inspiration from *Walden; or, Life in the Woods*, the 1854 treatise in which Henry David Thoreau offers a template for those who seek a transcendental escape into nature: "I wanted to live deep and suck out all the marrow of life, to live so sturdily and Spartan-like as to put to rout all that was not life, to cut a broad swath and shave close, to drive life into a corner, and reduce it to its lowest terms." He claimed that during his two-year project he found all four necessities of life—food, shelter (a 150-square-foot cabin), clothing and fuel—by growing vegetables and trading his labour, though he failed to mention that he was also regularly provided with food and laundry services by his mother and sister.

Thoreau has been labelled misanthropic, hypocritical and sanctimonious—the latter elevated to "inestimably priggish" by Bill Bryson in *A Walk in the Woods*—but according to Finkel, Knight's disdain for Thoreau was bottomless. Thoreau, he said, "had no deep insight into nature," having only spent two years at Walden Pond while his family helped him out. It's a peculiar perspective for someone who was not exactly living symbiotically with nature himself.

There are many paradoxical aspects to Knight and his hermitage: he rejected society yet chose to live as a social parasite; he traded his fear of human interaction for the fear and anxiety he provoked in his victims; he reserved his most bottomless contempt for an individual with whom he had much in common. Finkel suggests that Knight had no general disdain for humanity, but he untethered himself from it simply because it held no good spot for him. Finkel asks whether it would have been justifiable to "just give him a little bit of land, a few bags of groceries, and let him live peacefully?"

Was Bjornstrom, like Knight, driven to relocate to the bush as a refugee from society? Was he seeking a transcendental experience akin to that of Thoreau and McCandless? Or was he indeed thrust upon this path by an overpowering visceral reaction to events in his life—the Bre-X threats and stories of kids being harmed?

The last explanation would seem to be the most likely for his decision to walk away from the Rayleigh Correctional Centre with only six weeks remaining in his sentence. Otherwise, if his principal objective had been withdrawing from society or finding Thoreauvian transcendence, why not serve out the remainder of his sentence and avoid beginning his life as a hermit burdened by the increased attention of being a fugitive? Or, if he was just trying to get a jump on winter by heading into the bush at the end of September rather than in mid-November, why not walk away even earlier or serve out the remaining sentence, earn some money over the rest of the winter and start with more provisions than just a red prison sweatsuit? That would at least have put him further ahead than his previous, aborted attempt at a feral life.

Another inconsistency was the media attention Bjornstrom sought, which in itself shed further light on his rationale for trying to eke out an existence in the bush. In September 2001 he reached out to journalist Dale Steeves, who was covering the Bushman story for the newspaper *Kamloops This Week*. When Steeves persuaded him to meet in person a few days later at a location of Bjornstrom's choice, Bjornstrom asked him to provide a detailed description of himself and his vehicle and informed Steeves that he would be carrying both a rifle and a handgun. To get to the meeting spot, Bjornstrom had to hike for several hours, and he watched Steeves approach long before he made himself visible. "I'm the one they call the Bushman," he said as he appeared out of the bush to greet Steeves with a handshake. "John Lambert Bjornstrom."

He was wearing the green-and-black checkered coat stolen from the cabin owner whose wardrobe he favoured, along with ripped brown trousers over jeans, and well-worn high-top sneakers. As promised, he carried both a .357 handgun and a sawed-off .22-calibre rifle, and he instructed Steeves to walk on his left side as they hiked up a logging road. "I carry my firearms on my right side," he said. "We don't want to have an accident." When they reached a plateau overlooking Shuswap and Hunakwa Lakes, Bjornstrom proceeded to share details about his life as the Bushman.

He told Steeves he was prepared to do anything to evade capture, even if it meant shooting someone. He alluded to having various camps, enough propane to last until the following winter and enough canned food to last until February. "I will eventually go out and get more," he confessed. "The trouble is I have to break into places to get them. I have a great dislike for doing that." They discussed his upbringing, his various careers, his relationships and his kids. "It is hard to know you are a father and not be able to be there. You want to do something, but things have happened that you can't."

He said he started working for Bre-X after Walsh approached him, and that had led to investigating de Guzman's death: "I know de Guzman, the geologist who supposedly jumped out of the helicopter, was killed. De Guzman's death was planned. I was coming up with the information and ties to prove it." He said the individuals behind the murder were Indonesian businessmen and politicians. They had sent the men who ambushed Bjornstrom in his office, and followed that with the death threats that caused him to flee to the Shuswap the first time. He said that after his first sojourn in the Shuswap, he had been serving out his sentence in Kamloops when he received another threatening message connected to Bre-X, so he returned to the Shuswap to resume his "quest."

He mentioned his psychic gift and his belief that the Shuswap was being used for illegal purposes connected to organized crime. "They use the Shuswap for their purpose and their purpose is much worse than I can ever be," he offered up. "That's all I can say. Once I have got what I'm after here, I will leave. I will turn myself in."

He told Steeves that eluding the RCMP through the dense forest and over the rugged terrain was easy for him, and reiterated that victimizing cabin owners, which he acknowledged he would continue doing, was not. He said he was dispirited by loneliness at times and would yearn for companionship, but then he would step out of his camp, look around and affirm that he was not truly alone. "We are here, wherever we are, for a reason," he said. "There is a reason for everything and I believe there is a reason for me being here."

And then he disappeared back into the bush.

Tracy Hughes, who was covering the Bushman story for the *Salmon Arm Observer*, had contacted Bjornstrom by phone several times, usually on his cellphone but once from outside a fast food restaurant in Sicamous. When it became clear that Hughes, working for a small-town newspaper, could not manage the expense of interviewing him in person, Bjornstrom arranged for Ted Chernecki at Global News to do an interview under the condition he invite Hughes along to do her own story. The newspaper's lawyer cautioned her to avoid any possible implication that she was aiding or abetting a fugitive.

On a cold November day in 2001 the two journalists set off from Sicamous in a rented houseboat named the *Baby Jesus* to meet Bjornstrom at an agreed-upon location. A video of the Global News interview shows the *Baby Jesus* making its way up the lake while a Bushman song written by a local radio station plays in the background.

Two hours before reaching their meeting spot, Chernecki received a call from Bjornstrom to say that, even though they were still about twenty kilometres away, he could hear them with the underwater microphones he had installed in the lake. As they got closer to the end of Anstey Arm, he had them flash their lights and then directed them to a sandbar to beach the boat. He waited until he was sure they were alone before he approached by canoe and knocked on the houseboat door. He was wearing a wool sweater with a high crew collar under which he acknowledged he was carrying a .357 magnum pistol. They lit a fire, barbecued steaks and chatted about the night sky. When I contacted Chernecki, he recalled vividly that it was a clear sky and they had been treated to the spectacular Leonid meteor storm that occurs about every thirty-three years, made all the more brilliant without any light pollution—aside from some lights atop a nearby ridge that Bjornstrom kept an eye on.

The taped interview started with the three of them sitting on the beach around the campfire lit up by bright TV lights. Bjornstrom acknowledged that he was surviving largely off the backs of cabin owners and that if he'd been a victimized cabin owner himself, he would be as ticked off as they were. He said he regretted any damage he inflicted entering cabins, but that he was after a far greater evil.

Asked to describe a typical day, Bjornstrom said he usually began by checking his surveillance alarms, including the afore-mentioned microphones in the lake, which he had fashioned out of walkie talkie parts, monitoring them to make sure there were no boats on the water before he headed out. He showed them a video of one of his satellite camps that was about a two-and-a-half-day hike from their interview location. It was located high in the canopy, supported by four or five trees and capped with a large tarp with a rope ladder dangling below.

Other videos showed him sitting in a lawn chair, patrol-ling the lake with binoculars and what Chernecki described as a "German-made Kruger" in his lap (more likely the sawed-off .22), and riding a camouflaged dirt bike down a steep slope in camouflage clothing. He also told them he had a Ski-Doo, an ATV and several submerged canoes, including one with an "inboard" motor fashioned from parts he removed from an old Sea-Doo.

Another clip showed him in bed, reading a book and playing with a chipmunk while "Bridge over Troubled Water" played in the background. He later explained that a couple of chipmunks would visit him during brief breaks from their hibernation, and he made a box for them to play in inside the birdcage. (Some chipmunks do indeed semi-hibernate, waking every few days, raising their body temperature to normal, feeding on stored food, urinating and defecating before returning to their slumber.)

Bjornstrom told the two reporters about Bre-X—the henchmen, he said, "made their point quite well"—and missing children. Asked about his own children, he said there was nothing he could do for them at that time, and he was compelled to complete the task he had set for himself. "If I'm finished by next year, that'd be great," he said. "If I've completed it by winter, that'd be fantastic. If it takes five or ten more winters, then that's what I'll do."

Chernecki, who said he enjoyed the conversation—as well as subsequent conversations when Bjornstrom would call him collect from prison to chat—found Bjornstrom to be "fascinating as an individual and basically harmless." As the interview on the beach finished, he told Bjornstrom he'd prefer not to see him end up dead and asked if he would consider turning himself in, trading his life on the run for regular meals and a comfortable bed in prison. Bjornstrom responded that he'd rather die than return to prison against his will. The video concluded with Bjornstrom getting into his canoe—now covered with frost, as the temperature had dropped well below freezing—and paddling off into the night.

CHAPTER 13

HUNTING SEASON

▐▐ I know hunting season has started now, but from the way things are, it looks like I'm the big game."

John Bjornstrom

Sergeant Jim Harrison, who oversaw most of the effort to apprehend the "Great Shuswap Grocery Thief," as he refers to Bjornstrom, is unsuccessfully retired from the RCMP—they still recruit him for all sorts of assignments, allowing him only intermittent enjoyment of the retiree haven of Peachland, in BC's Okanagan Valley. Despite some inconvenience, he agreed to meet with me in nearby Kelowna. I was without a vehicle and grateful to him and his wife, Cathy, for being willing to drive nearly an hour so that he could meet with me while Cathy took their grandkids to the mall. It was the first tip-off to his good-naturedness, which I later confirmed with one of his former colleagues, who spoke of him in glowing terms.

When Harrison was transferred to the Sicamous detachment in early 2000, he took over responsibility for apprehending the Bushman. The departing detachment commander told him a crazy guy was living in the bush and committing the odd break and entry, and suggested that tracking him down might be a minor distraction from more pressing matters. By the spring, however, cabin owners were returning, and it became clear from the volume of break-in reports that it would be more than a minor distraction.

The RCMP detachment didn't yet have a boat equipped with radar, and infrared technology was not widely available, so Harrison and his team spent many hours bushwhacking with tracking dogs, using ATVs on the forestry roads, scanning from boats, even deploying a helicopter in search of the man. (Bjornstrom later recounted hiding inside his cave while the helicopter hovered so low he could smell the exhaust fumes.) "It's thousands and thousands of hectares of dense, steep bush, and we didn't even have a starting point," Harrison explained. He concluded that Bjornstrom was travelling the lake at night by canoe and covering large distances, and "it's obvious he's in tremendous physical condition." Harrison would sometimes patrol the lake in his own boat under cover of darkness, hoping to catch his nocturnal adversary commuting.

Visitors to the area found yellow posters on beaches and at trailheads stating that a fugitive was in the area and should be considered armed and dangerous: "For more information, contact any of the lakeshore residents, most all have been victims of his repeated robberies. You may be his next victim. If seen, contact Sicamous RCMP." According to one resident, most of the signs were removed within twenty-four hours, presumably by Bjornstrom himself. Nonetheless, potential sightings were relayed to the police, and the lakeside tranquility would be disrupted by the RCMP's Emergency Response Team (ERT) descending upon the area in full SWAT gear.

Meanwhile, pressure was building on the RCMP to bring him in. The mayor of Sicamous was apprehensive that tourists might be scared off, telling the media: "I hope that nobody gets the idea that they shouldn't come here because they'll be shot dead by the wild man." Criticism of the RCMP's approach was also mounting. "They have all this equipment and stuff. It can't be that hard to catch a guy out in the bush. They're going about it the wrong way," commented one confident local to the *Vancouver Sun*. "How would I catch him? You have to go live like him for a week or two, hang out there long enough. Send out three experienced bush guys and they'd have him located in a week. I know of two ravines myself. I don't know if the cops have gone down 'em."

The four law enforcement agencies tasked with taking down Christopher Knight, the North Pond Hermit of Maine, spent a quarter century conducting foot searches and flyovers before eventually apprehending him. It was ultimately a game warden named Terry Hughes who devised the successful trap after fruitless consultations with high-tech surveillance experts, private detectives and military acquaintances. Hughes's interest had been piqued by a conversation with some border patrol acquaintances who had recently returned from a training camp where they were introduced to new, closely guarded Homeland Security equipment.

Knight had been careful to avoid establishing patterns that could be detected, but perversely one of his favourite targets was the Pine Tree Camp Society kitchen that fed people with physical disabilities and their families. He had found a key to the walk-in freezer after they started locking it in one of several attempts to rebuff him. Confident he would return to the camp, Sergeant Hughes and the border patrol agents positioned sensors in a few locations in the kitchen and installed the monitoring unit in the sergeant's home. Just two weeks later the alarm went off in the middle of the night, and Hughes raced to the camp in time to see the beam of a flashlight spilling out of the freezer. As Knight exited the dining hall, he found Sergeant Hughes's Maglite and .357 magnum aimed squarely at his head.

Thirteen years before those sensors were used to capture the North Pond Hermit, the RCMP designed a similar trap to outsmart Bjornstrom, installing pressure mats in cabins throughout Queest Village that would be triggered when he entered and stepped on them. They set up a monitoring station in one cabin, the owner of which was responsible for notifying the RCMP when a cabin was infiltrated. However, there was one complication: whereas Sergeant Hughes was located close to the North Pond Hermit's targets, and he had practised responding to the signal to shave seconds off his response time, the cabins that Bjornstrom was targeting were far more isolated. When one of the sensors was triggered and the cabin owner notified the RCMP, they informed him they could be there the next day.

Frustrated, one cabin owner finally decided to take matters into his own hands, and one night when the alarm was triggered at a friend's cabin up the hill, he darted out the door, jumped in his vehicle and headed up the gravel road toward the cabin. As he approached, his headlight beams caught the windows of the cabin, and he could see a shadow moving quickly to the back door. He suspected he had startled Bjornstrom, who would now be heading for his canoe. The cabin owner decided to race him to the beach, but when he arrived, he didn't see a canoe or the telltale imprint a beached canoe leaves behind in the sand. Suspecting Bjornstrom might have left his canoe at another beach farther north, he phoned friends who had a view of that beach from their cabin to inform them they'd probably see him in about five minutes. They quickly positioned themselves by the windows and watched as the Bushman appeared briefly along the shoreline, silhouetted in the moonlight, before he paddled away.

The RCMP modified the trap by leaving bait bags in the cabins where the pressure mats were located. When Bjornstrom set off the pressure mat, they hoped he would take the bait bag, which contained items likely to attract him, along with tracking devices. ERT surveillance was established, and a professional tracker from the organized crime unit was brought in. The first time they thought they had him, the signal led them across the lake to a beach area and up a steep slope. When they reached the top of the slope, however, the signal died. Bjornstrom later left them a message to say that he had watched the whole operation. Another attempt to ensnare him failed when they found the bait bag stashed high up in a tree. There was no scent to follow either. "I covered all my tracks with a shot of bear spray," Bjornstrom later informed them.

The police left another package for Bjornstrom with a phone (unaware that he was generating his own electricity, they included an extra battery) and instructions to call an RCMP negotiator. They spoke a couple of times, and the negotiator also reached out to Bjornstrom's sister, but no progress was made.

Instead, Bjornstrom surprised Sergeant Harrison by calling him directly at home. Harrison explained to Bjornstrom that he would be captured eventually, and Bjornstrom politely disagreed. In time their conversations became routine to the point where the phone in Sergeant Harrison's house would ring, and he would hear his wife say, "Just a minute, John . . . Hey, Hon, John's on the phone for you." When Harrison tried to persuade his adversary to call him "Jim," Bjornstrom said he had too much respect for him and preferred to address him more formally.

Later that summer Bjornstrom reached a houseboat company by marine band radio and asked them to relay a message to the RCMP that he had left a package at one of the lakeside cabins. The RCMP found a tape recording in a bag hanging from the cabin's outside door handle. On the tape Bjornstrom requested another phone, a video camera, aerial photographs and pictures of two missing girls. He suggested that messages could be delivered to him via NL Radio, a Kamloops classic hits radio station he listened to, but the RCMP refused to communicate through the media. So Bjornstrom left another message to arrange a drop at a lookout about a ten-minute drive up a logging road from Queest Village. There are several boulders at the drop location, and they were to leave it on top of the one marked with the word *Fugitive* painted in large letters.

Bjornstrom had chosen the spot because he knew he could easily flee from it if he ran into trouble. The previous spring, he had been walking along the road when he came upon a cougar transporting her cubs one by one, gripping their scruff in her teeth. He had tried not to unsettle her as he continued along, but the affronted cougar gave chase, and he found himself trapped on the edge of a fifty-foot cliff. With limited options, he launched himself off the cliff and into a tree a little over ten feet away and slid down it out of harm's way.

The ERT members arrived a couple of days in advance of the drop date and stayed with a Queest Village cabin owner. Their eagerness to catch Bjornstrom was evident the first night, when they heard a boat on the water and "were outta here like a god-damned shot," according to the owner. They raced to the dock to borrow their host's aluminum fishing boat but were hung up by the daisy chain knot securing it and cut the rope in haste. Then they tore after the boat they had heard, perhaps not appreciating how uncharacteristic it would be for the Bushman to be that conspicuous. The couple in the boat, making their way home after a few drinks, were naturally alarmed when the ERT squad chased them down in the darkness.

The following day, the police left the requested items in a bag atop Fugitive Rock. The general duty ERT member, along with a sniper and a dog and its handler, camouflaged themselves in the bushes across the road. They expected Bjornstrom to arrive after dark, but he surprised them by sauntering down the middle of the road just after six p.m., his sawed off .22 slung over his shoulder. Bjornstrom had suspected the police would bring a dog, he explained in a later interview with the RCMP, in order to give themselves the advantage at night. As he made his way toward Fugitive Rock he heard the dog bark, and he disappeared over the cliff before he could grab the bag.

It wasn't a sheer drop below him, but it was a steep slope. Upon regaining his footing, he turned to see the dog in full pursuit. Knowing he would be in serious trouble if the dog hit him at that speed, or even worse, got its teeth into him, he stopped, turned and looked straight at the dog. It stopped but continued barking to hold him in place. When the handler, now also in pursuit, instructed the dog to continue pursuing, Bjornstrom turned and ran downhill, discharging bear spray behind him as he ran. The dog was only a few feet from its target when it was hit by the spray, and the handler, moving quickly down the steep slope behind him, was also unable to avoid the cloud of spray.

Aside from a few scratches, Bjornstrom carried on unblemished, but the thicket he found himself in was choked with obstacles, and he knew that a panicked run would likely lead him to trip. So he walked at a brisk pace down the remaining slope to the edge of the open meadow far below. The general duty team member tried to pursue him, but it was futile.

Thinking Bjornstrom might have a canoe waiting at the lake, the tactical team raced down to the Queest Village dock, startling many villagers in the process. They jumped into the same boat they had used the previous night, fired up the engine and charged down the lake, but he was nowhere to be seen.

The police decided against using the requested items to attempt another ambush and instead left them at another location for Bjornstrom to pick up with the intention of then tracking him through the phone. That was foiled when Bjornstrom, suspecting the phone was traceable, made a fake call and stashed a canoe nearby, leaving it visible to test whether it would be found. The next morning a boat carrying four people showed up to investigate the canoe, so Bjornstrom took the phone apart and disabled the tracking mechanism.

The situation was becoming volatile. Following the run-in at Fugitive Rock, Bjornstrom left a cassette recording in a cabin, and the message on it was allegedly given in a fit of rage. He called the RCMP "Keystone Cops" and said he was going to start shooting. Cabin owners were becoming increasingly agitated as well. Sergeant Harrison received a call one night from an owner who was watching from his deck as the Bushman paddled across the moonlit water.

"I got him right in the crosshairs. I'm gonna shoot him right now!" exclaimed the cabin owner.

"Put the gun down. We're on our way. Just put the damn gun down!"

"What if I just blow a hole in his canoe?"

"If you hit him, you'll be charged with manslaughter. Think this through!"

After putting the phone down, Harrison raced up to Anstey Arm in his own boat to see if he could catch Bjornstrom on the water but found only a tightly wound cabin owner.

Increasingly desperate, the RCMP devised a scheme that sprang from the media interviews Bjornstrom was conducting. They would pose as a film crew wanting to document his life in the bush. Two officers showed up at the house of Bjornstrom's sister Jennifer and introduced themselves as Woodrow Allen Scott (later shortened to Woody Allen) and Stéphane Sauvé, producers from *Real TV*, a television program that portrayed daring rescues, escapes, stunts and accidents. They claimed they were interested in producing a film on how Bjornstrom had survived in the bush and eluded police.

They asked if she would relay their interest to her brother and tell him he could reach them from a cellphone they had left for him at a location on the Shuswap shore. She was suspicious, having been visited several times by the RCMP and being aware that her land line was tapped. The next time she spoke with her brother—they spoke roughly every one to two weeks when he had a phone—he told her he had spoken to the documentary crew and had agreed to the interview under the condition that she come with the crew. She agreed to go, feeling that she should take advantage of this rare opportunity to see him. "I may not agree with what he does, but he's not a bad person," she rationalized.

On November 25, about two months after the initial approach, she flew to Kelowna, where she was introduced to a new member of the crew, Tim, and told that Stéphane had a family emergency to attend to. The three drove to Sicamous. The drive was unsettling for Jennifer: their questions made her suspicious about their actual motives, but she attributed her reaction to nervousness about seeing her brother again. By this point in the year most of the houseboats on the lake had been winterized and put up on blocks until spring—heavy snow loads can sink them if they're overwintered on the water—but the houseboat company did still have one available. It was the *Baby Jesus*, the same boat used by Chernecki and Hughes for their interview.

It was Jennifer's first time on a houseboat, and once they left the narrows at Sicamous and were underway, she gave herself a tour. After checking out the ladder to the rooftop lounging area, she smoked a cigarette and then returned to the passageway below and opened a door to a bedroom. Staring back at her from the other side of the bed was a man she didn't recognize, fully clad in black with a balaclava pulled up above his face. Upon seeing her, he immediately dove behind the bed.

Shortly thereafter, she received a phone call from her brother. The plan had been for him to suggest a meeting place once he was comfortable everything was proceeding smoothly.

"John," Jennifer whispered into the phone, "we're not alone." There was a pause in the conversation, but then he continued as if everything was fine and provided instructions to meet him. She assumed he didn't hear her, though it's possible he did and chose to disregard the warning so that his sister would not be charged with aiding and abetting him.

They continued motoring up the lake, Jennifer's apprehension growing now that she better understood the situation. They arrived at the meeting spot around three p.m., and after the front end of the boat nudged up to the sandy shore, Bjornstrom appeared in his canoe. Jennifer jumped from the deck of the houseboat and waited for him ashore, but when she gave him a hug, she felt a gun underneath his clothing. She suggested he get rid of any guns to avoid any unfortunate mishaps, which he did.

After motoring to another beach with Bjornstrom following in his canoe, the four of them moved inside the *Baby Jesus*, and Jennifer and her brother were seated by their hosts at the table. They proceeded to discuss the documentary while Tim mixed Caesars with pickled asparagus and Woody barbecued steaks, prawns and mushrooms. From her brother's responses to their questions, Jennifer could tell he was toying with them.

Around eight p.m., the dishes cleared, there was a ruckus at the gangplank. Suddenly a large man dressed in black appeared at the doorway carrying an automatic weapon in ready-to-fire position yelling "Freeze!" Jennifer recognized him as the one she had surprised in the bedroom. Following him was the rest of the heavily armed ERT team, their faces covered. Bjornstrom had just started eating a mandarin orange, and calmly continued as the ambush team surrounded the table and told him to raise his hands. "I'd like to finish my orange," he told them. Upon doing so, he got up and let them take him away.

The whole thing left Jennifer shaken, and she was apologetic when she hugged her brother before he was escorted to another boat. It was a long trip back to Sicamous, made worse for her because she was seated beside a growling police dog that left her terrified to move.

When they reached the dock in Sicamous, Sergeant Harrison was waiting. Bjornstrom was escorted from the boat to a police vehicle.

"Sergeant Harrison, I presume," Bjornstrom said as he was ushered past.

"Told you we'd get you, John," replied Harrison.

Jennifer was taken to a hotel, where she remained for a couple of days when her flight was cancelled due to a snowstorm. She caught footage on TV of her handcuffed brother being escorted into a police station. "Police did a good job," he said as he was released from a vehicle. A reporter asked him if it was true that a family member had turned him in, and he replied, "I guess you can't trust anybody." On returning home she had to face family members, including her widowed father, whom she was now looking after and who believed she had been away on a business trip. She was accused of having been paid off by the RCMP, and it took some time before everyone came to understand that she had been set up.

The Bushman's capture was of course a relief for Harrison, given the distraction the case had become. But, he told me, he was sad to learn about Bjornstrom's passing. "Different time and place, I probably would have gotten along great with John, because I love people and I love characters. People who dance to a different drummer are totally fine with me. They're just people. And I truly enjoyed that part of the experience. Looking back, what I got from John personally was that he was a character. In retrospect he wasn't a violent guy, he wasn't a bad guy per se. Yes, the things he did were bad, but not at the core of who he was. He wasn't a desperate criminal fuelling a drug addiction or out for personal gain—other than what he needed to survive." And then as an afterthought, Harrison added, "I'm not sure why he needed a toy boat in his cave."

CHAPTER 14

WHO'S LISTENING?

RCMP: Why would you have not finished that [six weeks in prison]?

Bjornstrom: Because of Bre-X.

RCMP: But could you not have come to somebody?

Bjornstrom: Because nobody was listening. I was speaking, but nobody was listening. And now you're listening more because of the episode that has taken place over the last two years. I mean, how far does a person have to go before people will actually listen?

When Jennifer Wells was researching *Fever*, she received an anonymous call that sounded eerily familiar: "I have some information regarding the Bre-X guy. I'm going to tell you the way it is. The body was dead in the helicopter. I know for an absolute fact he was dead inside the helicopter. He went out in a fetal position. I had a vision. Through the power of the Holy Spirit. I was gonna tell the RCMP but I changed my mind. I'm kinda on the outs with the RCMP."

The only inconsistency between that claim and Bjornstrom's claims was that Bjornstrom wasn't as absolute in his conviction that de Guzman was dead before he left the helicopter. In his interview with the RCMP after he was arrested in 2001, he claimed de Guzman "might have been dead at the time or just about there" at that point. However, the comment about the RCMP was consistent: Bjornstrom had been critical of the RCMP's investigation. He also noted elsewhere that the Holy Spirit "guided his hand." (That call wasn't the only one Wells received regarding alternative theories as she was researching her book. Someone calling himself "Jeff" spoke of the Indonesian government orchestrating the scam and cover-up. He told her, "There was a fourth person in the helicopter. Only five people in the world know what I know.")

It's one leap after another to believe that Bjornstrom could have concluded de Guzman was pushed from the helicopter based on some kind of vision, which in turn landed him on a hit list. But what if he did stumble upon a theory close enough to the truth that it panicked someone with influence and thugs were indeed dispatched to Calgary to impede his progress? That seems more plausible than the circumstantial evidence—the unknown man boarding the helicopter, the hit list, the threats—being fabricated by unconnected sources with no apparent reason for doing so.

There is, of course, no way to validate exactly what happened in Bjornstrom's office, so we will never know for sure what caused him to seek refuge in the Shuswap. It might be counterintuitive that someone would try to avoid a fearsome situation by living in the bush and travelling under the cover of darkness—a life that would surely terrify most modern-day mortals. Yet his initial, more conventional reaction of seeking assistance from the police only led to him being brushed aside.

His sister said he had often sought refuge in the bush from his visions—it was a wholly authentic refuge for him. So it follows that he would have escaped to the bush in this instance, given the burden of his visions. In his interview with the RCMP, he explained: "People who have psychic abilities, regardless of what it is, their line between sane and insane is much thinner than someone who does not have it." And he went on to argue that the further you cross over the line, the more you might bounce back the other way. Perhaps there was some Thoreauvian transcendence in him after all. "In the woods, we return to reason and faith. There I feel that nothing can befall me in life," wrote the author's mentor and the father of transcendentalism, Ralph Waldo Emerson.

The event at the Rayleigh Correctional Centre that prompted his return to the bush is, like the encounter in his office, difficult to confirm (the fact that the facility is no longer in operation being one hurdle). Bjornstrom told the courtroom during his trial that one day he recognized people watching the prison yard with binoculars from beside the adjacent road. Is it possible that they also fired two shots at him, as he told Rob Nicholson? It borders on inconceivable that the hired guns had returned and fired warning shots to deter him from pursuing his Bre-X theory any further upon his release—which is perhaps why he omitted the detail about the gunshots in front of the courtroom—but it seems he was at least given that impression. Whatever happened, something rekindled his panic, as he had otherwise conveyed his intent to serve out his nearly completed sentence.

He told the RCMP in his post-arrest interview that he wanted to return to the Shuswap to complete the investigative work that had drawn him there in the first place. Eventually his sixth sense was redeployed to that end, a process he likened to a horse being led by a halter shank. He said he found the skeletal remains of a man that he estimated had been there for fifteen to twenty years. He suspected the man had been sleeping under the stars, based on the bits and pieces of sleeping bag he found next to the body. Aside from some missing limbs, most of the skeleton was intact.

More alarming, he said, was a grave site he discovered in a clearing near an inactive logging road. The body was barely covered with earth, and he estimated it had only been placed there the previous fall. It was a female, about thirteen or fourteen years old, with dark hair that had been bleached blond. There were no obvious signs of how she had died. Nearby were two humps of earth, under which he found two more bodies that he estimated were also under sixteen years old and, based on the vegetation growth over them, had been there for five to ten years. He described returning to the site six weeks later to discover that the first body was now fully buried. There were tire tracks nearby, which he described on one of the cassette messages he left in a cabin as 16.5-inch tires on a three-quarter-ton truck. He also left hair samples in the bag that he hung from the door handle of one cabin along with a tape-recorded message requesting items from the RCMP.

After his arrest he was asked to show the RCMP the location of the graves, but he demurred, saying he feared he would become a target in prison: "Once you're in there considered PC [protective custody], you're garbage, the rats. So I don't want to fight my way through the prison system for survival." Perhaps because of his audience, he neglected to tell the RCMP something he had shared with others: his belief that one or more police officers were involved. He said he was committed to finding who had buried the bodies and had set up video surveillance from a nearby tree stand with numerous detectors that would transmit a signal to a marine band radio at his main camp if the perpetrators returned. As it was a two-day walk to the site, he stole the dirt bike to get there quicker. "It was tripped a couple of times," he told the RCMP, "and when I got to the place, it showed that it was . . . uh . . . elk."

Five months after he was taken into custody, the RCMP escorted him back to the area to identify the location of the bodies. Bjornstrom testified at his trial that he showed them the area where he discovered the exposed skeleton, which they suspected could have been the body of a missing hunter from many years earlier. He told them he had previously provided hair samples from the other bodies and reiterated his reluctance to disclose further information. The tension between him and the escorting officers was briefly defused on the return trip to Kamloops Regional Correction Centre when they stopped for dinner at a restaurant overlooking the Shuswap, and the staff took photos of the Bushman.

As the setting sun burnished the placid waters beyond the restaurant, and fun seekers enjoyed the last vestiges of daylight, his claims of finding bodies buried in the hills might have appeared all the more out of place. Yet the Shuswap has not been immune from the province's infamy with respect to missing and murdered women. The Missing Women Commission of Inquiry was established by the province of BC in the aftermath of the conviction of serial murderer Robert Pickton, who was believed to have murdered at least forty-nine women. Among other findings, the commission concluded that some of the features nature bestowed upon the province, including an extensive coastline, large wilderness areas and mild weather, have also contributed to the greater frequency of disappearances. Indeed, according to a recent investigation by the *StarMetro* and *Toronto Star* newspapers, 2,500 of the roughly 7,000 unsolved missing person cases in Canada occurred in BC, approximately twice the national average.

At Bjornstrom's trial, his lawyer, Don Campbell, presented a letter from a woman who had been contacted by Bjornstrom while he was in the bush and whose daughter was in her teens when she went missing from nearby Revelstoke in 1998. More recently, five women disappeared from the area during an eighteen-month period from 2016 to 2017. In one case, remains were found on a farm near Salmon Arm; the families of the other missing women continue searching.

Once again, I turned to Rob Nicholson for his perspective. He doesn't have any additional information regarding Bjornstrom's claims of finding bodies, but he does have a lot to say about investigating child abuse, including personal experience. His book, *Stolen Innocence*, self-published in 1998, describes organized child sexual abuse in BC, including incidents involving his own children, who he says were abused by his ex-wife and people she was involved with. Although initially licensed as a private investigator in 1993, he withdrew his licence in 1995 after bumping heads with the RCMP. He said that in a couple of instances he had duly notified them of his surveillance activities but that they exposed him to his surveillance targets, undermining his efforts and potentially exposing him to retaliation.

He continued to operate without an official license and as his investigative work expanded, he says he endured increasing resistance, including several bullets that narrowly missed him and threats against his family. It got to the point that he was putting Scotch tape on his car door to see if anyone had tampered with his vehicle. He says the threats culminated in a call from an individual who told him that if he didn't cease his investigations, the next time he saw his kids would be in a snuff movie. That was in 2005, and it was the end of his investigative work.

"Be careful when you write your book," was Nicholson's advice to me.

"Just to be clear," I replied, "what are you referring to specifically?"

"Child porn—that's mostly what I dealt with, and holy smokes!"

Nicholson told me that while he was still doing investigative work, he was contacted by individuals in the US who were retired from government service and were working on their own initiative to stem the flow of child pornography, of which Canada was a major source. That led him to the Shuswap. I tried to corroborate these statements, but statistics on child pornography are not readily available, other than tragic reports on the exponential growth of increasingly extreme material and a containment system at its breaking point. According to the National Center for Missing and Exploited Children in the US, in

2019 technology companies reported 69 million online images and videos of children being sexually abused. In 1998 there were three thousand.

After Bjornstrom's arrest, his first lawyer, Shawn Buckley, found himself in the unusual position of dealing with two individuals who were both investigating child pornography in the Shuswap area—and trying to protect themselves from Bre-X-related threats. Accordingly, when he needed someone to assist with validating Bjornstrom's claims of finding evidence of child pornography production, it was presumably an easy decision to turn to Nicholson. Buckley summoned the private investigator to a meeting in the warden's office at the Kamloops prison where Bjornstrom was being held. There, Nicholson learned that Bjornstrom claimed to have taken a few of the videotapes he'd found depicting child abuse, placed them in a cooler and hidden them with some other items in an eight-by-four-foot depression that he covered with a tarp and branches, roughly five hundred feet from a lighthouse on the north side of Cinnemousun Narrows. Nicholson was given the task of retrieving the cooler. The only person he could recruit to assist him was a friend named David Thomson, whom he describes as "a gutsy little fella who weighs ninety pounds soaking wet."

The two rented a twelve-foot aluminum boat with an outboard motor and set out for the lighthouse. It would have been a pleasant boat ride except that it was mid-December and the water was stirred up by a stiff headwind. Thomson told me he was huddled at the bow with his back to the wind while Nicholson sat in the stern, trying to maintain his grip on the tiller. Nicholson sensed they were being watched—a small plane circled overhead. Thomson, who was practically in fetal position trying to stay dry, says he was only aware of the plane because Nicholson kept talking about it. They made it to the reference point Bjornstrom had identified and spent the rest of the day doing a grid search of the area, but even though there was only a skiff of snow on the ground, they were unsuccessful. Their journey back, compounded by darkness, was even more uncomfortable.

Nicholson went back to Bjornstrom for more information and was told the cache was likely farther from the reference point than he had previously indicated, but it wasn't until the snow was gone that the intrepid boaters returned for another search. This time they decided to be more discreet and canoed to the location—an interesting rationale, as paddlers are more conspicuous on the Shuswap than motorboats. The trip took most of the day into a headwind, but they planned to stay the night so they would have plenty of time to explore the expanded search area.

Their search didn't take long: they were quickly alerted to the exact location because it was encircled by yellow tape. Ducking under the tape as if they were entering an active crime scene, they found the depression and within it many of the items Bjornstrom had described—tent, sleeping bag, plastic jugs. Only one thing was missing: the cooler.

Both investigations, into the bodies and the child pornography, led Bjornstrom to suspect police involvement, but he was reluctant to provide details, possibly because he didn't have any evidence, or maybe because he was apprehensive about potential repercussions.

His sister Jennifer told me she was aware of the identity of the individual who possessed the child pornography, but she was visibly shaken when I inquired further. Out of fear of retaliation, she was unwilling to divulge details.

Bjornstrom did not appear to have a grudge against the RCMP as he was eager to assist them in other matters. He directed them to a chop shop that he spent time surveilling near the Shuswap Arm, and numerous marijuana grow operations he stumbled upon around Anstey and Seymour Arms. He speculated that growing activity had diminished in the area due to his presence attracting greater police interest, but there were some substantial operations with elaborate gravity-fed water systems that the RCMP found noteworthy when Bjornstrom relayed details.

At least a couple of large seizures followed his arrest. One was in an area between Anstey Arm and Hunakwa Lake, where about two thousand plants were seized. Another, much larger bust occurred in 2004, at the end of Seymour Arm, when roughly 150 police officers descended upon the area one morning at dawn, outnumbering the full-time residents two to one. They arrived in patrol cars, unmarked Suburbans and a chartered houseboat that was used as a command centre. A helicopter circled overhead as SWAT teams fanned out in a four-kilometre radius to execute search warrants. In the end, they arrested sixteen suspects and confiscated growing equipment, more than twenty thousand plants and fifty weapons that they hauled away in rental trucks. As it was nearly a two-hour drive on a rough road back to the Trans-Canada Highway, some of the police officers stayed overnight with residents such as Alf Daniels, the owner of the local store, who was saddened by the likely drop-off in business following the arrests. "They [the growers] were buying stuff, buying food," he said. "I knew if they were shut down, we'd lose money here at the store. I was on good terms with them. I never had any worries."

According to Sergeant Harrison, none of these marijuana busts stemmed from information provided by Bjornstrom. Regardless, it reinforced the idea that he was predisposed to working with the police. In fact, he later acknowledged to the RCMP that he had wanted to be a police officer himself: "We're on the same team. I did what I had to do in order to survive. If I had to do my life all over again, if I had the choice to be a cop, there would be no question."

CHAPTER 15

DELUDED DELUSIONS

> ❝ I don't think that somebody that spends five months carving a cave
> out of pure rock is just simply doing it for the gratification of people
> liking him."
>
> **Don Campbell**, Bjornstrom's lawyer, speaking to the media in
> 2004 before Bjornstrom's trial

It became immediately clear to me upon entering Don
Campbell's law offices in Kamloops, located in a nicely repur-
posed house in a central neighbourhood near the courthouse,
that the Bushman had been a memorable client. A black-and-
white courtroom sketch hung on a wall outside the office,
depicting Bjornstrom, in a shirt and tie, standing behind
Campbell in his barrister's robe. Inside the office a similar
sketch, in colour, adorned a wall, alongside gifts from various
First Nations and pictures of Campbell enjoying his hobbies.

They were all adrenaline-seeking pursuits—freestyle skiing, paraskiing, scuba diving, skydiving and BASE jumping,

including a jump off the iconic El Capitan in Yosemite National Park that landed him in jail for a night—that became an antidote to the stresses of being a defence lawyer. Most of the photos on his walls showed him formation skydiving, which he started doing in the 1990s. The objective is for a group of skydivers, typically four to sixteen of them (the record being four hundred), to complete as many formations as possible within a specified period of freefall time. The pinnacle of Campbell's participation in the sport came in 2012, when at age fifty-four he competed for Canada in the eight-person competition at the world championships, held in Dubai. Part of the attractiveness of formation skydiving, particularly for an ageing adrenaline junkie, was the sport's low-impact nature compared to prior extreme sports that had taken more of a toll on his body.

When the discussion eventually turned to Bjornstrom, Campbell quickly confirmed that he had indeed been a memorable client, and he dug out some poems Bjornstrom had written for Campbell's daughters, along with thank-you letters and a Christmas card. "Not only was he the most amazing and interesting client I ever represented but by far the most interesting person I have ever met," he offered. "I'm actually not convinced he was a real person."

According to Campbell, most of his clients were path-of-least-resistance criminals. They didn't want to get up early and work a regular job; they got up at noon, stole a few things and bought some drugs. Bjornstrom was totally different. He also differed from typical clients in his trustworthiness. Campbell believed that nearly all his clients lied, and did so regularly, often just to avoid cognitive dissonance. Bjornstrom was the total opposite, to the point that Campbell came to believe everything he said.

Bjornstrom told Campbell about his work with street kids in Calgary and their claims that child pornography was being filmed in the Shuswap area and some kids were even disappearing. "Normally you would just take that information to the police, but the kids kept coming back with stories that the police were somehow involved in it," Campbell said. "It sounds crazy, but shortly after the trial there was a police officer at a Shuswap detachment who was implicated in child pornography."

Not only was Bjornstrom like no other but, according to Campbell, representing him attracted some unprecedented and unnerving attention. Throughout the whole process, there was a constant stream of troubling things that didn't make sense: regular clicks on his phone line, correspondence that had been tampered with. "I'm the antithesis of a conspiracy theorist," he told me. "My preference is to say there's a rational explanation for all of this. People don't care enough to conspire. They're too busy just getting through their day. But there was so much weird shit that happened that it was almost inescapable that there was something going on."

Undeterred, Campbell pressed on with preparations for the trial. The prosecutor was pushing for a six- to eight-year sentence for his client, arguing that a longer sentence was necessary partly because Bjornstrom had suggested to the Crown-appointed psychologist that as soon as he was released, he intended to return to the Shuswap to continue his pursuit. Indeed, Campbell acknowledged that his client believed to the "depth of his cellular being" that he had a mission to complete.

Nothing could change that resolution, neither the significant hardships he would continue to face if he did return nor the prospect of a shorter sentence if he agreed to stay away.

When he initially took on Bjornstrom as a client, it looked like a trial could take a month or two, which was enticing from the prospect of both remuneration and publicity, but ultimately his client was going to get convicted by the evidence. "I don't recall if there were ten or twenty B&ES, but there were a shitload of B&ES," he said, "and while you might be able to throw out 20 per cent of those by finding a problem with the evidentiary trail, it wouldn't make a difference at the end of the day. He would still get a serious jail sentence."

It took Campbell many hours to convince Bjornstrom that fighting the charges would not put the focus on his crusade. The prosecutor would instead portray him as a scary, terrifying, nasty criminal. "The Crown won't call in witnesses who will say, 'Thanks for looking after my property or boarding up my place after some kids broke in and vandalized it,'" Campbell told his client. And a trial would revictimize everyone he stole from. It would be day after day of people speaking to their fear, how they had felt violated and hadn't felt safe since.

Campbell also tried to persuade Bjornstrom that returning to the Shuswap likely wouldn't do much for his ultimate objective either. To the extent there was something nefarious happening to kids, it had likely been flushed out by the publicity attracted to it by Bjornstrom's activities. In Campbell's eyes the perpetrators Bjornstrom was after were also path-of-least-resistance people, and the people most impacted would be the innocent ones who would be revictimized. Pleading guilty would demonstrate his honourable intentions and shift the focus as much as possible to why he had been there. This would be the most effective way of keeping his crusade alive.

Eventually Bjornstrom agreed and pleaded guilty to ten charges that included break and entry, uttering threats and extortion. The sentencing trial in January 2004 began with a submission from the Crown prosecutor, Gregory Koturbash, who listed Bjornstrom's previous convictions; noted that the crimes in question were committed while he was at large from the Rayleigh Correctional Centre, where he was serving a sentence for identical crimes; described the impact his threats had on victimized cabin owners; and enumerated the cost of his actions, not just for cabin owners but also the hefty cost incurred by the RCMP in their efforts to apprehend him. He argued that any remorse shown by Bjornstrom should be measured against his intention to return to the Shuswap to continue searching cabins for evidence. Furthermore, he cautioned that Bjornstrom's stories of Bre-X and criminal activities against children in the Shuswap area had to be treated as delusions, based on the lack of evidence.

Testimony from some of the victims followed. They spoke of the inconvenience of their property going missing and, more troubling, the trauma of having their personal space violated and the concern for their safety. "I feel foolish admitting that I sleep with an axe by my bed," testified one victim, "but without it, I wouldn't sleep." Another described sleeping with a butcher knife under her pillow and eventually avoiding the place altogether while Bjornstrom was at large. Another was particularly unsettled by a message Bjornstrom left on a cassette tape saying that one night he had enjoyed listening to her dinner table conversation from outside her cabin. "I don't think that I'll ever really feel the comfort there that I felt before we were broken into," she said.

According to Campbell, lawyers are normally reluctant to risk giving potentially unbalanced clients an opportunity to speak at a sentencing trial, as they're likely to "say crazy shit that doubles their sentence," but he was confident that it would be worthwhile to let Bjornstrom speak. His testimony began by responding to questions from Campbell about his life in the bush and the circumstances leading up to it. He told the court calmly that he had been searching for evidence of child pornography and abuse. He found "tidbits of information," not enough to establish the presence of an organized operation but too much to rule out its existence.

He confirmed that he broke into roughly thirty cabins to obtain supplies but said he was also looking for evidence of child pornography or connections with missing kids. He argued that he was not responsible for all the break-ins, and when he came across ransacked cabins, he did his best to repair doors and windows to keep animals out. "I didn't want to add insult to injury," he said. He acknowledged the fear he had stoked with some of the notes and tape-recorded messages he left but claimed that any threats he made were attempts to keep people from pursuing him and causing themselves harm. "They were victims. I agree and apologize for that. But what I said then and what I would do were two different things. I know I was out of hand, but I didn't want to frighten people."

Koturbash began his cross-examination by probing Bjornstrom about his life in the bush. "You'd agree with me that you're a fairly strong individual to be able to do something like that?" he asked, referring specifically to the tree stands that

Bjornstrom had explained he built to look for abnormal comings and goings involving children.

"I was in good fitness, yes," Bjornstrom responded.

"And you knew the area like the back of your hand?"

"No, every day was something new to learn. I mean, there were new spurs, new trails, new roads—or old roads that have long since shown their signs of use. I did the best I can."

"You knew the area better than most? You were able to avoid the detection of the police for almost two years in that area?"

"Yes, but that's not hard," Bjornstrom said. "The police are not bush people. They're street people."

"Okay. And you'd regard yourself as a bush person?"

"No, but I maybe regard myself as being experienced in the bush."

Koturbash suggested Bjornstrom was motivated by seeking fame. "They had written a song about you and played it on the radio?"

"I found that humorous, yes."

"But you did feel important. People were paying attention to you?"

"I feel important all the time."

"You felt more important because people were paying attention to you?"

"People were paying attention. If I had planned this, it would never have worked out this way. How the media and everything got started, it's all an accident. It's nothing that I went out of my way to arrange on purpose."

"Does it excite you that someone wants to make a movie about you?" Koturbash asked in reference to a proposal by a Vancouver production company.

"I'm tickled, yes," Bjornstrom replied.

Next Koturbash challenged Bjornstrom's claim to have psychic abilities and to see auras. "What do you see right now around me?"

"Light blue."

"And what does that tell you about me?"

"That you have a light blue aura," said Bjornstrom, prompting an eruption of laughter from the full courtroom.

"Don't ask him what he sees around me, counsel," said the judge.

Koturbash questioned Bjornstrom on the number of guns and amount of ammunition he took. "Over one thousand rounds of ammunition, that's quite a surplus for not using your firearms very often."

"Yes."

"What were you expecting to happen, Mr. Bjornstrom?"

"I have no idea."

"You seem to have a fascination with firearms, isn't that true?"

"I have a fascination for fishing poles, too."

When asked why he had refused to lead RCMP to the burial sites, Bjornstrom contended that he didn't trust the police.

"It's because [the burial sites] don't exist, isn't that correct?"

"They do exist," replied Bjornstrom, who later identified the locations on a map in the courtroom.

Koturbash was able to get Bjornstrom to acknowledge the impact of his extortion attempts. "You thought about, 'What would make a person scared [enough] to comply with my demands?'"

"I didn't want to break into cottages."

Kortubash repeated his question: "You thought about, 'What would it take to scare a person enough to comply with my demands?'"

"I didn't think of the receiving end of it, no."

"You didn't need the food to survive. You told us that you knew how to hunt, how to fish, how to eat the vegetation."

"Yes."

"In fact, you ate and drank pretty well off the backs of the cabin owners, didn't you?"

"I admit it, yes."

When Koturbash contended that without proper treatment Bjornstrom was a threat to reoffend, he based his argument on Bjornstrom's prior admissions that he intended to return to doing what he had been arrested for. On the stand, however, Bjornstrom stressed that he had no intention of returning. When pressed further on the issue, he staunchly confirmed his intentions. "I said I'm not going back—I'm not going back."

Campbell had hired his own psychiatrist, Dr. Stanley Semrau, to complete interviews with Bjornstrom and conduct an exhaustive review of police and court files and other psychiatric reports. He concluded that Bjornstrom may indeed have had personality disorders—paranoia and narcissistic tendencies, intense attachment to unusual ideas—but he was not delusional, had no mental disorders and posed little risk to the community. He told the court, "There's an element here of an idealistic commitment to what he saw as being an extremely important issue, and indeed, I mean, no one would debate that, you know, dealing with missing children and unsolved murders and child pornography is an extremely important societal problem, something that needs to be dealt with. But his particular personality characteristics resulted in his approaching those issues with a degree of commitment and idealistic obsession that is vastly greater than you would see almost anyone else pursue them."

To add perspective, Semrau gave examples of how personality traits that can be viewed as disorders in some circumstances can be beneficial in others—including his own wife's view that characteristics beneficial to him as a psychiatrist, such as being an excessive organization freak and somewhat narcissistic, weren't always as useful at home. In his opinion, lawyers often have one or two personality disorders, and the really good ones sometimes have more—for example, grandiosity, obsessive-compulsion, narcissism. "I would think that we have a good one-third of the population in round numbers who have enough in the way of problematic personality traits that they struggle with them," he said.

"The kind of energy and enthusiasm and commitment and perseverance which Mr. Bjornstrom has demonstrated, channelled in more productive and effective directions, is one of the key things that makes some of the most valuable people in our society . . . So you wouldn't want by any means to turn Mr. Bjornstrom into some sort of bland person who didn't care about much except what's on TV this evening. I mean, that would be a crime to do that," Semrau argued. Furthermore, he said that in his view Bjornstrom exhibited above-average personal characteristics typically seen as more desirable, including that he was "ruthlessly honest" and showed a total lack of guile. "Certainly it was my impression that he strongly believed the things he was telling me."

When Koturbash responded by asking how Bjornstrom's beliefs, which he insisted had to be considered delusions, could be sequestered through treatment, Semrau questioned whether that was a legitimate objective to begin with. He stated that true delusions have no basis in reality and aren't shared by anyone else. In contrast, Bjornstrom's claims were made in a logical manner that mirrored facts, and more tellingly perhaps, he expressed opinions shared by others, including Semrau himself. "I'm aware of things that the public isn't even aware of in general," he said, "of major police corruption investigations." And he questioned how Bjornstrom's claims of what happened with Bre-X could be labelled delusional. "I happen to believe myself that someone did kill Michael de Guzman, okay. I mean I had some Bre-X shares and, you know, I paid a little attention."

Semrau continued by saying that delusions are not necessarily negative as long as they don't lead to dangerous anti-social behavior. In some instances, they can even help people live happier lives, "as long as the individuals do not harm themselves or others." Even as he acknowledged that Bjornstrom undoubtedly engaged in anti-social behavior, Semrau argued that he displayed no violent tendencies and that any threats relayed through notes or audiotapes were "tactical tools" as opposed to intentions.

Koturbash next challenged Semrau on whether Bjornstrom was likely to reoffend, or as Campbell paraphrased: "We know he's dangerous without treatment, he hasn't had treatment, ergo he's dangerous and must go to jail."

The psychiatrist countered that prison programs could do little for someone with Bjornstrom's unique psychological makeup. Furthermore, he argued that during the two years the Bushman had been locked up awaiting trial, he had effectively received treatment from Campbell himself. Through those conversations, he had come to appreciate that returning to the Shuswap would be a counterproductive way to continue his crusade. "He has now, I think, shifted considerably in terms of the intensity of his felt need to pursue his concerns in a no-holds-barred kind of way," said Semrau. "He is of the view now that he's sort of done what he can and that the torch kind of needs to be passed to other people who might pursue things, not especially the police, you know, but other people with interests such as his who would be prepared to sort of investigate and research things and so on. He also already expresses the appreciation that it simply has not been fair and decent to cabin owners to damage their places, to steal their things, to cause them to be in states of fear and to lose enjoyment of their property. That it's simply not a fair and decent thing to do and that, furthermore, it hasn't been effective."

Justice Metzger ultimately agreed that Bjornstrom wasn't a threat and handed him a conditional sentence. His decision noted that Bjornstrom may have believed he was engaging in a law enforcement enterprise, but that belief did not cancel out the illegality of his methods. At the same time, the judge believed Bjornstrom would make an honest attempt at modifying his anti-social behaviour on his own and that the prison system had little to offer him in that regard.

Bjornstrom was sentenced to twenty-three months' house arrest and three years' probation and also given a number of conditions. In Campbell's opinion it was a remarkable decision, given the six to eight years sought by the prosecutor. (When first arrested, Bjornstrom himself had suspected he might get nine to fourteen years.) Given that he had nowhere to go, as he had been living alternately in the bush and a jail cell for over four years, he was directed to live with his sister Jennifer in Williams Lake to serve out his house arrest.

Campbell's family joined him outside the courthouse after the verdict. His wife and three daughters had become close to Bjornstrom who, according to Campbell, was "super friendly" to them. One of his daughters asked Bjornstrom for their auras, and Campbell indicated to Bjornstrom that he could go ahead—while at the same time murmuring under his breath something about it being horseshit. "He points at my daughters and goes purple, blue, green. That really rattled me, because they were the same colours they had chosen to paint their rooms. 'Who is this guy?' I kept asking myself."

According to Campbell, Bjornstrom left jail as a healthy, gentle soul who just wanted to work. "The fact that someone like him exists is totally incompatible with what we understand about people." He said it was one of the few cases out of the thousands he had taken on that was truly meaningful to him and confirmed his sense of why it was important to represent clients the right way. In parting, Bjornstrom agreed to join him for a canoe trip around the Shuswap after his conditions expired, but it never happened.

Sadly, Campbell died in a skydiving accident in October 2019. He was memorialized for his extensive work with clients who struggled with addiction, homelessness and mental illness and found it difficult to get the representation they were looking for. "He would put up with an awful lot of stressors to serve those people, and he served them well," a colleague told Kamloops TV station CJFC.

After Bjornstrom's release, it wasn't long before he was forced to return to court. When he met with his parole officer in Williams Lake—who, according to Jennifer, was clearly enthralled by the publicity surrounding Bjornstrom—he was told that his only restriction was that he check in occasionally. Two weeks after his release, Jennifer asked him to pick up a bottle of wine, as she had invited friends over for dinner. Someone spotted Bjornstrom, who rarely drank, in the liquor store and called the police, who showed up at Jennifer's home and reluctantly told her they had to take him in.

Back in court, there was a debate about whether the roughly twenty conditions of his sentence were sufficient. The probation officer and the Crown also expressed concerns that Bjornstrom had been offered an opportunity to appear in a television commercial for Kokanee beer. At the time, the beer company's advertising campaign centred upon a fictional ranger and the "Glacier Girls"—three young women typically dressed more for the beach than for a glacier—who were deputized to track down an elusive sasquatch who stole Kokanee beer. It was a trivial exercise, visualizing the Bushman as a stand-in for the sasquatch. The court decided that it didn't constitute "approved work," and he was sent back to live with his sister, this time with an electronic ankle monitor.

CHAPTER 16

INTO THE LIGHT

> A heart of gold is a treasure
> A heart of gold brings but little pleasure
> All mankind possesses a heart of gold
> But a heart of gold can turn cold
> Now a heart of love is a pleasure
> A heart of love is a pleasure we can treasure"
> **John Bjornstrom**

Bjornstrom was not the only forest-dwelling fugitive to be labelled "the Bushman." The Bushman of Pitt Lake—the same lake that Bjornstrom had run away to as a youth and that served as a foyer to the Lost Gold Mine—was a man named Peter Hunt. According to the RCMP, he had British military training in bush survival and was prone to violence, and it was the latter that prompted the original Bushman to label him a thug unbefitting of the name.

Hunt began stealing from cabins around Pitt Lake in 1999. The RCMP nearly arrested him once, but he bear-sprayed them and tried to steal one of their guns before getting away. He also shot at local residents who had initiated vigilante efforts to hunt him down—they had even established a command post—before he was arrested in 2000 in a Vancouver suburb.

A week after he was released on parole in 2003, the RCMP received calls that a man suspected of stealing from cabins around Pitt Lake had been sighted. ERT members and local police donned camouflage and staked out the lake, resorting to night-vision goggles once darkness fell. In the middle of the night they spotted the suspect in a canoe and gave chase in their motorized boat. Hunt tried to out-paddle them, but eventually succumbed to the futility and surrendered.

Two years later, the serial offender was again out on parole and tried, yet again, to outmanoeuvre the police. This time he had stolen a Sea Ray motorboat as well as a motorized inflatable in the suburb of Port Coquitlam. When the inflatable was spotted on the Fraser River, the police took to the water in a Zodiac and enlisted the help of tugboat operators to be on the lookout. Shortly after two a.m. a tugboat operator spotted the stolen boat and the police gave chase, but Hunt accelerated, narrowly missed them, beached the boat nearby and fled on foot. Apparently he had anticipated the possibility of being chased by the police again, as he was dressed in camouflage and carried smoke bombs, but the police, unfazed by his incendiary distractions, quickly captured him behind a dumpster.

Few additional details are available on the other Bushman, so it's unclear what his motives were and, indeed, how much time he even spent in the bush (according to one report, he actually lived on a houseboat). While awaiting trial for his own crimes, Bjornstrom was relieved to learn about his counterpart's arrest. "I'm glad he's not out terrorizing somebody," he told a reporter. "You're supposed to be able to go to the cottage to have fun."

I didn't ask any Anstey Arm cabin owners for their thoughts on that remark, but I feel safe assuming many would question its sincerity, as they felt Bjornstrom had robbed them of their fun. Worse than that, some lost so many possessions that the Bushman became more than just a nuisance, and for some the irritation had morphed into terror, with the prospect of further break-ins exacerbated by threatening letters and tape recordings.

I can relate. My family's cabin, located farther south, was plundered by a group of drifters around the same time. They used it as a base for several days while stealing from other cabins in the area, and in their idle time they defiled the place. They wrote obscene messages on the mirrors, busted up furniture, emptied food on the floor and overfilled the sinks. Even kids' art books weren't spared from graphic and chilling additions. When they left, they took everything they could easily remove, including bedding and utensils.

As they tried to make their exit, one of the wheels on their vehicle slipped into a hole and they were unable to extricate it. When they sought assistance from a neighbour, he was immediately suspicious and phoned the police, but by the time they arrived, the trio had stolen a van from another neighbour, transferred everything from the stranded vehicle and fled. Given the brashness of the crime, we couldn't help but wonder if we had been targeted for some reason. The police eventually apprehended one man, a drug addict with a criminal record, which only partially diminished the lasting impact their assault had on the sanctity of the place.

Bjornstrom never ransacked any cabins, but some of his threats had a similar impact. He seemed to appreciate the threat he posed, acknowledging that he too would be disgruntled to be victimized in such a way, and he showed regret for having felt compelled to do so. He also showed an interest in developing a relationship with the cabin owners and seemed disheartened when they couldn't appreciate his valiant watchdog efforts, both to protect cabins from other threats and to eradicate more nefarious activities. Presumably that's why he didn't think he had inhibited anyone's fun.

The note he left that stuck with me the most was the one saying how he enjoyed watching the progress one family's kids were making at waterskiing. It was easy to see how that was perceived as a ghastly threat. Yet, having more knowledge of who he was, it seems to me much more likely that he was legitimately interested in the kids' progress and was just attempting to establish a connection, albeit in a painfully awkward way. That was certainly the view of his family members, who concurred that he couldn't hurt a fly. Sergeant Harrison eventually came to the same conclusion: "He was a character—a very polite character—and in his mind he had no intention of hurting anyone. There wasn't a mean bone in his body. At the time though, I had to assume that he might."

Back in Williams Lake after being released, Bjornstrom resumed driving cargo trucks and also worked as a tow truck driver. One of his employers said he was a good worker who stayed on the job until it was finished, didn't back away from any challenges and always fixed things that went wrong, or at least attempted to. He preferred to be on his own and particularly enjoyed jobs that took him farther afield. He also started a limousine service on the side with his sister, and sometimes on special occasions he would treat friends and neighbours to a ride in the limo. Jennifer thought he looked cute in his chauffeur's uniform and black driving cap. She also remembers telling him his beard complemented the outfit—the only memory she has of lying to him. She still firmly believes that he never lied to her.

His release from jail was covered by the national media, and Lucette, his first romantic partner, happened to catch footage of it in Ontario. She tracked down his lawyer's number and sent a message asking if he could forward her number to Bjornstrom. It wasn't long before they reconnected, and after a few months' communication, he asked her to join him in Williams Lake. She agreed and shortly thereafter moved in with him and his sister, a temporary solution until the court agreed to a change of address and the reunited couple could find a place of their own. They got along surprisingly well, she says, and he gave her anything she wanted. They were set to be married, and Don Campbell, Bjornstrom's lawyer, was to be the best man. "I asked her to marry me in 1989—she just took a long time to answer," he told a local newspaper. Alas, it didn't come to be. People can change over the course of twenty years, Lucette told me, and feeling too far from family, she eventually returned to Ontario.

I asked if she had a sense of what guided him and where he derived his sense of morals. She said he wasn't religious, though his poems do contain references to the Christian Trinity. His interpretation of the Trinity, the mystifying three-in-one God, recognized the three persons as being distinct.

The Holy Spirit as a guiding force:

> The Holy Spirit guides my hand
> and quenches my soul.

Jesus as the role model:

> We must not forget our maker,
> and keep Jesus as our Hero.

And the Father as the gatekeeper:

> When I stand before God,
> and he questions my task,
> with Jesus and his Ghost (Holy Spirit),
> I have no question to ask!!

He also drew inspiration from a more unlikely muse: Tupac Shakur. Several of his poems referenced the rapper, who became a symbol of resistance and activism against inequities, and Bjornstrom drew parallels between their lives. The following is a poem from the collection he sent to his lawyer:

> Tupac where are you . . .?
> your shadow is growing faint,
> Are you still a thug,
> about to become a saint . . .?
> The flavor of your music,
> spices up my rhyme.
> You too were an outlaw,

convicted of a crime.
Your book of poetry,
about the rose and concrete.
Inspired this ballad,
and took me from defeat.
You died way too young,
you paved a way from pain.
Tupac the rap star,
forever you will reign.

The book of poetry referenced in the poem, Tupac's *The Rose That Grew from Concrete*, was written when the rapper was still a teenager. The title was taken from a poem in the collection that paid homage to a rose that was able to grow out of the sidewalk, "when no one else even cared." The book was published after Tupac was murdered in 1996 at the age of twenty-five, shot four times by a still unknown assailant in a drive-by shooting in Las Vegas.

Bjornstrom became concerned with the inequities in Williams Lake and devoted some of his time to the local Salvation Army, which is located on a central street corner, the upstairs dedicated to a thrift store and the lower level reserved for a soup kitchen. Even though the economy in that area relies on a relatively diversified set of industries—forestry, logging, sawmilling, mining and ranching—the city is not free of poverty and homelessness. Bjornstrom visited the soup kitchen biweekly, usually bringing coffee, cookies, donuts and jokes. The woman who runs the soup kitchen told me he has been missed since he passed away and described him as a jolly guy whom everyone enjoyed being around. At Christmas, she said, he would help arrange gifts for everyone and dress up as Santa to hand them out.

In 2014 he decided he wanted to take his public service further, and he ran for mayor on a platform of improving economic development, including greater diversification of the local economy, and crime reduction. The latter was focused on the eruption of youth gang violence in and around the city. One of his suggestions was a jobs program that would recruit gang members to complete some of the district's neglected projects.

Asked by the local media about whether his own criminal misdeeds were a political liability, he said: "I admit it and I've paid my dues. Once you buy something and you've paid for it, the payment is done." At the same time he viewed his backwoods savvy as transferrable to political savvy and joked about using the slogan "Bush sense makes good sense." He also felt he could relate to a wide spectrum of people, having "been at the bottom end of life and at the top." On election day he finished last with only 91 out of 3,433 votes. Nonetheless, he had put himself out there again to help marginalized members of society.

This leads to the question that troubled me the most as I navigated the circuitous path Bjornstrom left behind: how was he able to reconcile his desire to look out for others with seemingly not doing the same for his own children? When asked a similar question at his trial, he had said, "It's not hard for a man to be a father, but I find it takes someone special to be a dad. I don't quite get to be that special."

Before reaching out to his daughter Julie to get her perspective, I deliberated on how to communicate the appropriate amount of empathy on the presumably sensitive topic of her relationship, or potential lack thereof, with her father. I'm sure my Facebook message was still awkward, so her prompt response was all the more unexpected: "I would love to talk to you. I miss him dearly."

I met up with her in the town where she lives, Smooth Rock Falls, which is down the road from Kapuskasing in northern Ontario. I had only one option for a place to stay, the Moose Motel, and one option for breakfast, Smoothy's, which is where I sat down for a lengthy visit with Julie. I never met her father, but there was no mistaking her as his daughter.

She said he wasn't in her life in her early years. As a toddler, she would ride past his place in her grandparents' car and point to his horse and ask to go and see it, unaware that it belonged to her father or that she even had a father. Then one day when she was four, her grandparents told her she had a father, that the horse, Charlotte, was his and that she could meet both. "We bonded instantly," she said about their first encounter, which involved a horseback ride. "We've always had a very strong connection." They began seeing each other every other week. At first it was difficult to communicate, as Julie spoke only French at home, but the language barrier disappeared once she started school.

After Bjornstrom moved to Calgary and around the time he was fleeing to the Shuswap, Julie left home on her own adventures, which began with a program at the Oklahoma State Horseshoeing School. She was following in her father's footsteps as a farrier, though she says she didn't appreciate that at the time, but she was also escaping something, just as her father had: her stepsister, with whom she was very close, had committed suicide earlier that year. Her mother, Lucette, attributed the suicide to scars from childhood sexual abuse, and based on comments Bjornstrom made to her, Lucette suspects her daughter's experience may also have motivated him.

After completing the horseshoeing program in Oklahoma, Julie moved to Texas, where she fell for a Texan and for a horse. "It's a good place for a gypsy because of the horses. It fulfills you." One small fiery red mare in particular caught her eye, though Julie wasn't able to purchase her at the time. A year later, when the image of the horse wouldn't leave her, she called the owners, and they told her they had sold the mare just the day before. The next day she saw her husband leaving with the horse trailer, and he returned with the fiery red horse, Sugar. From that day forward, Julie and Sugar were never far apart.

Shortly thereafter she and her husband had a daughter and then a son. For various reasons she felt she couldn't stay in Texas, and she returned to southern Ontario with her son before coming back to Smooth Rock Falls to look after her ailing grandparents, who had largely raised her. Her grandfather passed away a few years ago and her grandmother more recently, capping off a tough year in which she also lost her father and Sugar.

Julie says her "gypsy blood" has never stopped stirring, but she's aware of the sense of abandonment that followed her father—and herself to some extent—and is determined to provide more stability for her seventeen-year-old bull-riding son. (She has other dependents, including cattle, horses, rabbits, dogs and cats, and although her son has been processing the cattle, she says the other critters aren't going anywhere.) She does emergency dispatch work from home and represents country music acts on the side. Meanwhile, her daughter has the same love for horses and an even more natural way with them, and is surrounded by them in Texas.

Julie was in touch with her father throughout his escapades, receiving collect calls from him during his first jail stint in Kamloops and then calls from the cave, though she wasn't aware he was calling from a cave at the time. When he was arrested the second time, some of his former horseshoeing clients saw him on TV and notified her. "It didn't shock me," she said. "He was highly intelligent, but he didn't always choose to use it the right way. Sometimes it's the highly intelligent people that do the stupid stuff."

After his release he continued to check in on her regularly and seemed to sense when she needed uplifting. "Hey, doll, are you okay?" he would ask. Beyond letters (later replaced with text messages), he sent many gifts, including books, movies and cowboy boots for her and the grandkids. The most cherished thing he sent her was the saddle he first left home on, which had been stored for him by one of the ranchers he had worked for. She said she can relate to him in many ways—she has even tried trucking—and might have lived an even more similar life if circumstances had allowed.

"I wish I had his will to survive in the bush," she said. "I'd probably go to the bush too, where it's peaceful. People make mistakes. It doesn't mean they're bad. He wanted people to understand that people are still worth it. We're all human beings. You have to believe in them. If you stop believing in people, then I think those people eventually give up on themselves."

According to Bjornstrom's sister Jennifer, as he grew older, he yearned for a stronger relationship with his children and grandchildren. That was especially true as he became sicker and sensed he didn't have long to live. In his final year he was beset with diabetes, ulcers, heart issues and failing lungs. She felt he never recovered once his health started degenerating, because he didn't want to burden anyone by asking for assistance, though he was still keen to help others and stayed behind during the Williams Lake fire to look after friends' animals and property.

He spent his final days in a motorhome parked in the yard of friends, who would check on him regularly. One frigid February morning they went to feed the chickens and found him face-down and frozen on the ground, an empty bucket in his hand, presumably on his way to collect water.

"I didn't think he would die so young," Julie reflects. "He had a joy for living. If he did give up at the end, his spark had died." When he fell ill, he asked her to join him, but she was preoccupied with looking after her ailing grandmother, so she never saw him in his final days. She finds solace in the relationship they did have, which both of them cherished, and in the fact that he did not need much to enjoy life. "In a way he lived an exciting life because he loved simple living."

Indeed, based on his poetry, it would seem he found the light before the end:

> Do you know where you're going . . .?
> I've been there and back.
> Now I'm into the light,
> and out of the black.

With luck, according to Margaret Atwood, the writer is also able to bring something back out to the light after entering the darkness. The thing is, Bjornstrom's cave wasn't actually that dark—there was a light switch, after all. Questions may have multiplied since I was first compelled to peer inside, but any darkness seems to have resided elsewhere.

ENDNOTES

Endnotes cite sources that provided one or two specific details; for more general sources, please see the Acknowledgements section.

CHAPTER 3: THE CALL OF THE BUSH

14 between 250,000 and 1.5 million Roma were executed by the Nazis: G. Csanyi-Robah et al., "The Devouring: It's Time to Recognize Roma Genocide," *The Globe and Mail*, August 2, 2016.
15 over thirty-seven thousand Hungarians were welcomed to Canada: J. Beaudoin et al., "No Refuge: Hungarian Romani Refugee Claimants in Canada," Osgoode Legal Studies Research Paper Series no. 12/2015.

CHAPTER 4: STARGATE

23 In 1995, for a special program called *Put to the Test*: L. Weeks, "Up Close and Personal with a Remote Viewer," *Washington Post*, December 4, 1995.
24 Their findings were tempered by the lack of evidence: M. Mumford et al., "An Evaluation of Remote Viewing:

Research and Applications," American Institutes for
Research (1995).

CHAPTER 5: GILDED DREAMS

35   would divest $56 million of Bre-X shares in total: Based
on class action lawsuit Carom et al v. Bre-X Minerals Ltd.
et al (1999), 98 OTC 1 (SC).

CHAPTER 6: GILDED GREED

38   When Jakarta's water system was privatized: B. Koerner,
"How Did Suharto Steal $35 billion?," *Slate*, March 26, 2004.

38   The state oil company, Pertamina, had roughly 170 contracts: T. Friend, *Indonesian Destinies* (Cambridge, MA:
Belknap Press, 2003), p. 251.

38   When the company was audited in 1999: T. Carroll and D.
Jarvis, eds., *Asia after the Developmental State: Disembedding
Autonomy* (Cambridge: Cambridge University Press,
2017), p. 243.

41   Hasan and Suharto met when Suharto was a junior army
officer: C. Barr, "Bob Hasan, the Rise of Apkindo, and
the Shifting Dynamics of Control in Indonesia's Timber
Sector," *Indonesia Journal*, Cornell University Southeast
Asia Program, vol. 65 (1998).

41   After a round with Sylvester Stallone: R. Pura, "Plywood
Power: Bob Hasan Builds an Empire in the Forest," *Asian
Wall Street Journal*, January 20, 1995.

41 He had just recently settled a dispute between two of
    them: "Indonesia's Uncle Bob," *Economist*, March 27, 1997.

42 paying for vacations and college educations for some
    of their children: J. Perlez and R. Bonner, "Below a
    Mountain of Wealth, a River of Waste," *New York Times*,
    December 27, 2005.

42 even though insurance held by the company had recently
    been revoked: R. Bryce, "U.S. Cancels Indonesian Mine's
    Insurance," *New York Times*, November 2, 1995.

CHAPTER 7: THE SORCERER

50 Alo and Puspos blamed it on the air conditioner and
    photocopier: "FIA Interim Report of Investigation
    into Tampering with Bre-X Minerals Ltd. Busang
    Core Samples," Forensic Investigative Associates,
    October 3, 1997.

55 ". . . it is very sensitive. It is close to the son of our leader":
    J. Stackhouse, "New Crew Piloted de Guzman's Helicopter,"
    The Globe and Mail, April 5, 1997.

55 Tursono's testimony was later revised: M. Saragosa,
    "The Mine, the Man, and the Scam," *Asiaweek*,
    November 30, 2000.

CHAPTER 8: AFTER THE GOLD RUSH

63   Investor Lawrence Beadle: D. Baines, "Vancouver Man Killed Self Over Bre-X Decline," *Ottawa Citizen*, May 9, 1997.

63   And a guilt-ridden stockbroker named Pierre Turgeon: B. Hutchinson, "Dead Losses," *Canadian Business*, May 29, 1998.

64   "I'm quite comfortable that I know how it happened": T. Seskus and S. Wilton, "Why the RCMP Didn't Get Their Man," *Calgary Herald*, May 28, 2007.

64   Court filings showed his estate was essentially bankrupt and faced a $33 million charge: P. Waldie, "Tax Department Panned as Walsh Case Thrown Out," *The Globe and Mail*, June 23, 2008.

66   She has her own theory regarding de Guzman's death: P. Waldie, "Ingrid Felderhof Weighs In on the Bre-X Scandal," *The Globe and Mail*, July 29, 2007.

67   He'd had plenty of time to reflect on what happened at Busang: T. Saywell, "John Felderhof's New Life After Bre-X," *The Northern Miner*, December 26, 2012.

68   The man who completed the autopsy: S. Wilton, "Bre-X: The Real Story and Scandal That Inspired the Movie *Gold*," *Calgary Herald*, January 30, 2017.

68   Genie, the second of de Guzman's wives, believes he is still alive: Ibid.

72   Some family members hired Dr. Jerome Bailen: Ibid.

CHAPTER 9: THE HIT LIST

81   For example, Tommy was caught making a minor side deal: K. O'Rourke, *Reformasi: The Struggle for Power in Post-Soeharto Indonesia* (New South Wales: Allen & Unwin, 2002), p. 233.

81   Tommy was questioned as a witness: Ibid, p. 377.

82   Tommy was sentenced to eighteen months in prison: "Suharto Son Fingered in Assassination," *Ottawa Citizen*, August 8, 2001.

CHAPTER 10: SKOOKUM TUMTUM

91   Dawson travelled great distances throughout Canada's west and north: *The Journals of George M. Dawson*, ed. D. Cole and B. Lockner, vol. 1, *British Columbia 1875–1878* (Vancouver: University of British Columbia Press, 1989).

92   On his first trip, in 1877, he surveyed the region: D. Marshall, ed., *Photographic Memory: Salmon Arm's Past in Essays and Pictures* (Salmon Arm: Okanagan Historical Society, 2007), p. 34.

CHAPTER 11: HUNAKWA

115   a tree's girth isn't actually correlated with the wind speed required to topple it: E. Virot et al., "Critical Wind Speed at Which Trees Break," *Physical Review E* 93, vol. 2 (2016).

115   Entire sections of the Canadian Pacific Railway had to be altered: "Devil's Club," Sierra Club BC, accessed March 2, 2020, https://sierraclub.bc.ca/devils-club/.
118   Sockeye salmon operate on a four-year cycle: "A Salmon Journey: "From the Shuswap, to the Ocean, and Back Again," Adams River Salmon Society, accessed March 2, 2020, https://www.salmonsociety.com/journey/.

CHAPTER 12: OFF THE BEATEN TRACK

127   the Coyote Camp people travel through the southwestern US: H. Jacobs, "Meet the Contemporary Hunter-Gatherers Who Live Off the Land in the American West," *Business Insider*, December 14, 2017.
128   author Jon Krakauer assembled a team of scientists: J. Krakauer, "How Chris McCandless Died: An Update," *New Yorker*, February 11, 2015.
129   Finkel suggests that Knight had no general disdain for humanity: S. Worrall, "Why the North Pond Hermit Hid From People for 17 Years," *National Geographic*, April 9, 2017.

ACKNOWLEDGEMENTS

As this book was going to print, I learned that Jennifer Bjornstrom had passed away from natural causes. I was unable to finish a discussion with her regarding donating a portion of the royalties to charity—our conversation awaited her reading an advanced copy of the book that was sitting in her mailbox—but I was able to receive feedback from others. Ten percent of author royalties from sales of *The Bushman's Lair* will be split between the Canadian Centre for Child Protection and the Shuswap Trail Alliance. I hope she and John would have approved.

Writing this book was made possible by the contributions of many people. I am indebted to those who were close to John and shared intimate details: Julie, Jennifer and Lucette. Rob Nicholson went well beyond selling me documents and became a valued resource. Sergeant Jim Harrison, even having already devoted many hours to the Bushman, went out of his way to help me. Jim Cooperman not only guided us through the Shuswap backcountry but shared his well-earned insight into everything about the Shuswap and reviewed a copy of the manuscript. My lengthy meetings with Don Campbell took time out of his busy schedule and solidified my interest in telling this story.

I am grateful for the support of family and friends, in particular my parents, who were devoted team members and supporters. Manders provided valuable assistance and is of course a great travelling companion. Abbie Coros provided encouragement to write this book at the outset in the form of a pivotal ultimatum.

Navigating the publishing world felt like my own version of surviving in the bush, and I am very appreciative of author Stephen Bown for his eagerness to guide me through it. I would also like to thank author David Berrade for providing early encouragement and feedback on the manuscript.

I would like to thank Harbour Publishing for taking a chance on this book, and particularly Anna Comfort O'Keeffe for investing her wisdom and patience. Peter Norman did a masterful job of editing, and I will miss working with him. Thank you as well to Marisa Alps, Anna Boyar, Corina Eberle, Charlotte Gray, Berglind Hendrickson, Teresa Karbashewski, Betty Keller, Rebecca Pruitt MacKenney, Shed Simas and the team at ZG Stories for their contributions.

For providing feedback on a sensitive topic, and for their hospitality, I would like to thank the cabin owners of Anstey Arm who shared their experiences. Some wished not to be named, so I have avoided using any names.

For information on John Bjornstrom, I benefited from coverage by journalists Ted Chernecki, Mike Cornell, Marnie Douglas, Petti Fong, Cam Fortems, Michael Friscolanti, Tracy Hughes, Robert Koopmans, Rod Mickleburgh, Chris Nuttall-Smith, Larry Pynn, Gwendolyn Richards and Dale Steeves.

For information on Bre-X, I benefited from books written by Vivian Danielson and James Whyte; Diane Francis; Douglas Goold and Andrew Willis; Brian Hutchinson; and Jennifer Wells.

For information on the Shuswap, I benefited from books written by Gwen Bauer and Estelle Noakes; Jim Cooperman; Deanna Kawatski; and Denis Marshall.

Thank you to Charlie Mackenzie for allowing me to use the words to his song "Bushman of the Shuswap," available on most streaming services, and for providing some early encouragement.

Valuable contributions were also made by Melani Bradford, Ted Chernecki, Ryan Cicansky, Graham Farquharson, Brent Judd, Brian King, Martha O'Connor, Jenn Okrusko, Tamara Robinson, Nick Sheremeta, Cindy Studer, David Thomson, Stephanie Ward, Martha Webb, Peter Weisinger, Jennifer Wells and Suzanne Wilton. To Stephen Bown, Alex Hutchinson, Grant Lawrence, Stephen Legault and Lynn Martel, thank you for being early readers and for your support.

Lastly, my greatest thanks goes to my family: my wife, Kylie, who was probably tempted to send me to live in a cave to do extended research, but instead chose to embrace this endeavour with love, support and inspiration; and our children, Carson, Myles and Molly, who are a very bright source of light.

CREDITS

Lyrics from "Bushman of the Shuswap" by Charlie Mackenize, released on February 2, 2018, reproduced with permission of Charlie Mackenzie.

Excerpt from *Negotiating with the Dead: A Writer on Writing*, by Margaret Atwood, reproduced with permission from Cambridge University Press through PLSclear.

Excerpt from *Survival: A Thematic Guide to Canadian Literature*, by Margaret Atwood, copyright © 1972 by O. W. Toad Ltd. Reproduced with permission from House of Anansi Press Inc., Toronto.

Excerpt from *Bushcraft: Outdoor Skills and Wilderness Survivial*, by Mors Kochanski, reproduced with permission from Lone Pine Publishing.

My Way

English words by Paul Anka

Original French words by Gilles Thibault

Music by Jacques Revaux and Claude Francois

Copyright © 1967 Societe Des Nouvelles and Editions Eddie Barclay

Copyright © 1969 Chrysalis Standards, Inc. and IWay Holdings SAS

Copyright Renewed

All rights for Chrysalis Standards, Inc. administered by BMG Rights Management (US) LLC

All rights for IWay Holdings SAS administered by Concord Copyrights c/o Concord Music Publishing

All rights reserved

Reprinted by permission of Hal Leonard LLC and Alfred Publishing LLC